PENGUIN CANADA

WRITER'S GYM

ELIZA CLARK is the author of the novels *Miss You Like Crazy* (shortlisted for the Trillium Book Award and the Stephen Leacock Medal), *What You Need* (nominated for the Giller Prize), and *Bite the Stars*. She has taught creative writing classes for over a decade, most recently at York University in Toronto. She co-directs an online writing workshop and manuscript editing service (www.thewordlounge.com), and works as a television director.

Writer's GYM

Exercises and Training Tips for Writers

ELIZA CLARK

PENGUIN
CANADA

PENGUIN CANADA

Published by the Penguin Group

Penguin Group (Canada), 90 Eglinton Avenue East, Suite 700, Toronto, Ontario, Canada
    M4P 2Y3 (a division of Pearson Canada Inc.)

Penguin Group (USA) Inc., 375 Hudson Street, New York, New York 10014, U.S.A.
Penguin Books Ltd, 80 Strand, London WC2R 0RL, England
Penguin Ireland, 25 St Stephen's Green, Dublin 2, Ireland (a division of Penguin Books Ltd)
Penguin Group (Australia), 250 Camberwell Road, Camberwell, Victoria 3124, Australia
    (a division of Pearson Australia Group Pty Ltd)
Penguin Books India Pvt Ltd, 11 Community Centre, Panchsheel Park, New Delhi – 110 017, India
Penguin Group (NZ), 67 Apollo Drive, Rosedale, North Shore 0632, Auckland, New Zealand
    (a division of Pearson New Zealand Ltd)
Penguin Books (South Africa) (Pty) Ltd, 24 Sturdee Avenue, Rosebank, Johannesburg 2196,
    South Africa

Penguin Books Ltd, Registered Offices: 80 Strand, London WC2R 0RL, England

First published 2007

(WEB) 10 9 8 7 6 5 4 3 2

Author representation: Westwood Creative Artists, 94 Harbord Street, Toronto, Ontario M5S 1G6

Dave Eggers's exercise was adapted from *Don't Forget to Write*, a collection of lesson plans
benefiting 826 Valencia.
Copyright © 2006 by Ron Carlson. Used by permission of Brandt & Hochman Literary Agents
Inc. All rights reserved.
Original manuscript page from *Buying on Time* by Antanas Sileika. Used by permission of the
Porcupine's Quill. Copyright © 1997 by Antanas Sileika.

Pages 187–88 constitute an extension of this copyright page.

Manufactured in Canada.

ISBN-13: 978-0-14-305427-6
ISBN-10: 0-14-305427-9

Library and Archives Canada Cataloguing in Publication data available upon request.

Visit the Penguin Group (Canada) website at **www.penguin.ca**

Special and corporate bulk purchase rates available; please see
www.penguin.ca/corporatesales or call 1-800-810-3104, ext. 477 or 474

CONTENTS

FOR WORKSHOPS AND WRITING GROUPS

MORE WRITER'S GYM EXERCISES

INTRODUCTION

The plan for the *Writer's Gym* was always to keep it simple. Here are tips, techniques, books to read, methods to try. Just as one element of fiction flows into the next, all working together, the *Writer's Gym* can be opened to any page for inspiration. With a single exception, all the contributions are original to this book. All are offered in the same spirit. Other how-to books may get you thinking about writing and talking about writing, but when you want to actually write, this book will get you *doing* it. Here, some of the best coaches are in your corner. Flex your muscles. Be playful. Write and knock us all out.

Writer's GYM

FIVE RULES FOR WRITERS

Douglas Coupland

1. **Stop writing to impress your Lit 400 prof.** Readers can smell it from the first sentence, and the *last* thing your lit teacher wants to see is a successful student. It's the most jealous profession on earth.

2. **Write every day.** Only hacks write when the spirit moves them.

3. **Finish the goddamn book.** Every year I meet maybe twenty people writing novels and not one of them has ever finished one. That's three hundred novels across fifteen years. Finish the book and you're practically published already.

4. **Getting published doesn't change your life.** If you're writing because you think being published will change your life in some way, stop immediately, because nothing changes.

5. **Do you sound like yourself?** If a committee of people who know you were given a thousand samples of writing and were asked to tell which one was yours, could they do it? If not, keep working.

Bonus advice:

6. **Dreams are boring.** Don't write about them.

SUGGESTED READING

I don't want to give the impression that these are my ultimate three books, because they're not, but each crystallizes some important aspect of writing:

Appointment in Samarra by John O'Hara: dialogue, dialogue, dialogue.

Winesburg, Ohio by Sherwood Anderson: braiding a collection of narratives together to create a whole.

Play It as It Lays by Joan Didion: a masterpiece of minimalism.

Three excellent books in any event.

INTERVIEW
Rick Moody

Whose writing taught you how to write?

Mostly things that are about beautiful prose, like Samuel Beckett, James Joyce, Herman Melville, Virginia Woolf. Stanley Elkin, Bruno Schulz, Jorge Luis Borges, and Lydia Davis are also good examples. And I'm not sure they taught me how to write, but they taught me to dream big, and to trust my inclinations. I learned how to write through a lot of trial and error.

How do you begin the process of composition?

I don't think I begin the same way every time, so it's hard to say. Sometimes it's an image. Sometimes it's a character. Sometimes it's a line of prose. With my recent novel, *The Diviners,* I had the first sentence kicking around in my head for a long time before I started the book. It was a sentence that made me want to push forward. Sometimes that's enough to start a whole book. One meager little sentence.

What is the biggest challenge for you in writing?

First drafts. I know I can always finish something if I manage to get through the first draft, but that's sometimes quite hard. I don't always want to do it. Like many writers, like many people (!), I am sometimes lazy about getting down to work. I don't always want to do it. Once I get there I'm fine and am pretty prolific. But I actually have to sit down at the computer.

There's a fine line in your work between tragedy and comedy. How do you approach writing emotional scenes?

All colors come from the same color wheel. All moods are close together. The one tone shades into the next. I just let the emotion happen. I don't like narratives that are sentimental or melodramatic, and I don't think it's my job to affirm the tender truths of humanism. That's for greeting card writers. Perhaps because of this, the emotional palette in what I do is often subtle, which people occasionally mistake for a lack of strong feelings. The truth is that I just don't like garish displays of sentiment in fiction. Or in life, really.

You said once that "genre was a bookstore problem." How important is nonfiction in your fiction?

Less and less important. Lately, I like making things up. I stand by my remark, however. In the James Frey era, fiction and nonfiction are intimately related whether we want them to be or not. But having said that, I have no more autobiography to tell, which means I am free to invent. And I like inventing.

How would you describe your style of writing?

Maximalist.

Do you set challenges for yourself with each book? Would you give some examples?

Yes. I get bored easily. I like to try new things. I still believe in the modernist ideal that the novel is not exhausted, that the novel can do whatever it wants, whenever it wants, without having to explain its motives. Fragmentation, disjunction, collage—these are good strategies. Modernist strategies. You'd be surprised what an unpopular notion modernism is these days. Formula rules the roost. But I get bored, unfortunately, so I try new things, despite the unpopularity of this manner of working. Examples? I figure there are a lot of them in my work. I almost always have a formalist notion undergirding what I'm working on. In *The Diviners,* the idea was to structure the book episodically, as in a television series, or in an eighteenth-century novel. With the next book, I have a further idea in mind, an elaboration of structural ideas implicit in *The Diviners*. And so forth. I don't know if this is the right way to work, and sometimes I wish I was just storytelling. But this is my way of approaching the work, and I can do no better than work the way it's given to me to work.

How do you feel about the books you've written—your body of work as a whole?

I see it as somewhat restless, impatient, ambitious. But I am proud of these kinds of impulses. My only regret is that *Garden State* is a piece of shit. But I couldn't do any better back then.

Why do you feel that way?

I think any person who has written or thought about writing or is ambitious in this direction could see why *Garden State* is a piece of shit, and it's hard for me to bear down on the question, because it depresses me too much. But in brief let me say that the book is blunt, artless, desperate, and the storytelling is appallingly primitive. It's not lived in. It's both distant in a kind of artificial way and so harrowingly vulnerable that I for one intend never to look at it again. I feel about it sort of the way you feel about your fucked up younger brother during his third trip in rehab. You love him, you sympathize, you're sorry about the whole mess, but you hope he doesn't darken your front step now or in the future.

What is the best part of writing?

Absolute liberation.

What advice would you give to a new writer?

That the better part of the job is patience. Well, patience and temerity. People who want instant results are in the wrong line of work. So be patient, and don't worry about results. Worry about the process. The results will take care of themselves. There will be results of some kind.

ADVICE FROM THE GURU

Margaret Atwood

I was crouching in the mouth of my cave the other day, gnawing on a bone. It was one I'd gnawed before, but we folk have a way of repeating our themes and motifs, and in my defense I must say that my manner of gnawing this bone was ingenious, creative, and inventive, or at least it seemed so to me. The fully gnawed bone, when presented for inspection—at bone-gnawing fairs, competitions, and the like—would be judged a tour de force. Or so I hoped.

As I gnawed away, diligently as ever—you can't be a good bone-gnawer without putting in the work, inspiration isn't enough—I saw a young person approaching, clambering up the steep hillside that leads to my modest dwelling.

My dwelling is modest as an example. Although bone-gnawers may indeed generate considerable income over the course of their careers, this is not typical of them. Indeed, unless they renounce the accumulation of pelf as their main goal and dedicate themselves to their art, they will never rise above the level of plastic scrimshaw.

I watched the progress of my visitor, wondering who it might be. Just in time, I remembered that it was one of my consultation days. I do this consulting work as a favor to the youth of today: *To you from failing hands we pass the torch,* so to speak. Or the bone. I like to think that when I'm no longer around, the ancient bone-gnawing rituals will continue on the same as ever. With novel flourishes and fashions and so forth, of course, needless to say.

Hastily I donned my consultation outfit. It's a black veil with crystal beadwork on it, very imposing; it covers up the unimpressive jogging pants and sweatshirt I actually wear to do my work. No point in getting bits of gnaw all over your dressier vestments.

I laid out my skull and candle on a small side table, and fumbled around with the matches. Setting and costume plausibility are very important, I often tell my consultees. Slip up on the appropriate veil, pick a fraudulent-looking skull, and you've lost the viewer's trust.

The traveler came nearer. I shall not reveal its gender: I want everyone reading this to be able to Identify. They tell us these days that this business of Identification is important, though we old gnawers never used to bother with it. In those days identification was up to the viewer, not the gnawer.

I got the candle lit just in time. "Hail, stranger," I said, sepulchrally.

The person of tender years seemed properly in awe. "Hail, Great Bone-Gnawing Guru," s/he said. Well, somebody'd been taught their manners, anyhow.

"Wherefore seekest thou me?" I said.

"What?" The hair-free visage wore a puzzled frown. Languages of all kinds—verbal, visual, musical—do have a habit of changing over the years; it's necessary for those in our trade to recognize that, and to employ each idiom as fitting.

"What the fuck do *you* want?" I growled. The juvenile was immediately set at ease.

"I want to learn to be a master bone-gnawer, just like you," s/he said.

"You cannot be a master bone-gnawer *just like me*," I replied. "Each master gnawer is unique and produces work that could not have been made by anyone else. You must learn to be a bone-gnawer just like *yourself*."

"But how do I do that?" asked the bewildered neophyte.

"See this jar?" I said. It was an empty jam jar. I keep a supply of them handy.

"Yeah."

"You need to put your soul into it. Then screw the lid on tight, so it can't get out."

"My what?"

"Your soul. You need to keep your soul handy, where you can get at it. Then, when you've done enough practice—when you're ready to create your first gnawing masterwork—you need to pour some of your soul onto the bone you're gnawing. Not all, don't waste it. You don't want to use up all of it on just the one bone."

"But I don't believe in souls!" said the callow personage. "I didn't come here to talk about shit like that!"

"Then what *do* you want?" I said. They always react like this when I mention souls.

"I want you to give me some tricks of the trade," said the youngster. "At your age, you must know a lot of them! Hints about how to get my work displayed, what I need to do to promote it, building my self-confidence, overcoming gnawer's block, working with form and structure, that kind of thing. How to win big prizes. You know, the important stuff."

"All those things might be discussed," I said. "They are worthy topics for exploration. We could deal with craft—when to use the incisors for swift, telling bites—incisiveness, you might say—and when, on the other hand, to resort to a slow grinding motion, or a meditative chomping and chewing. Variety is important, as is rhythm. Or I could suggest some networking techniques—do you have an agent?—or make some comments on your methods of ornamentation and arrangement. But none of it will be of any benefit unless you can accomplish the one thing needful."

"The one thing …?"

"You need to be able to take the gnawed bone," I said, "which is a dead thing, as we all know," I added, "a useless sort of thing, really," I elaborated, "*qua* gnawed bone," I annotated, "and make it come alive. Unless you can do that, your work will remain inert. Maybe it will look good—it may have a sort of ossified polish, a gleaming, calcified magnificence even, but it won't do anything. It will just lie there. It won't dance."

"Dance?"

"Making the dead bones dance," I said. "That's our real trade. The gnawing part is just preparation; it's a sine qua non—excuse me, a necessary factor—but it's not an end in itself. The dancing of the bones—that is our true desire. That is our art."

"But how do I go about making the—what you said?" queried the postadolescent, with a hint of impatience, or possibly desperation. Some people, of course, can't tell a dancing tibia or ulna from one that's dead as a doornail. Such are bound to have trouble. I must add that twitching and jerking, as opposed to dancing, are different motions altogether.

"I told you how," I said, sadly, but with a certain mordant empathy. "That's what the soul is for. First of all, though, you have to find it. That may take you some time. And I must warn you that of all who set out on that momentous quest, only a few succeed. Some never find their souls; others do find them, but spill them, or break the jar. Still others trade them in for something more practical. Or sell them."

"Sell them?" said the youngster, with a mercenary gleam in her/his eye. "For a lot?"

"Good luck to you, my child," I said rather tersely. "You'll need it."

After s/he had parted from me, not altogether politely—"Piss off, you batty old creep," were the words I believe I heard—I decided to make myself some tea, before going back to my gnawing task. Thirsty work, this giving of advice. Not that it isn't fine advice, as advice goes.

Ah, if only I myself could always follow it!

PRETEND YOU'RE A BLIND CAT
Gail Anderson-Dargatz

When we were first dating, my love Mitch Krupp said to me, "You're a very sensual woman, aren't you?" It wasn't for the reasons you imagine. Well, it was for the reasons you imagine. But at that moment what he was getting at was that I was forever tasting things, touching things, listening to things, smelling things, and then talking about those experiences with him. "Smell that?" I asked him, squirting the zest of an orange peel on to his lips. "Taste it!" I said.

I love Mitch's personal scent, and I decided that my character Jude in my upcoming novel would smell like him. It was a familiar smell, one I recognized from somewhere else but couldn't put my finger on. So one day I hit on the idea of smelling every jar in my spice rack to find it. There, in my own kitchen cupboard, I stumbled on to his smell: cumin.

In *Inside Memory*, Timothy Findley tells about how, when he was writing *Not Wanted on the Voyage* and trying to gain the perspective of one of its characters, who happened to be a cat, he was caught at the beach on his hands and knees sniffing the rocks. A family came by and assumed he was a drug addict on a binge and told their kids to stay away, then debated among themselves whether or not they should phone the police. "As soon as they were gone," he wrote, "I got to my feet and ran up into the trees. What if these people really do call the authorities? What will I say? I was just pretending to be a blind cat?"

What has all this weird smelling and tasting got to do with writing? Like Timothy Findley, I believe a writer must be willing to embarrass himself in the pursuit of the world and everything it has to offer. If I, as a writer, can engage my senses and emotions, then I can engage my reader's as well.

■■■ THE EXERCISE ■■■■■■■■■■■■■■■■■■■■■■■■■■■■■■■■■

So, my exercise is a simple one: Go sniff everything in the spice rack. Run your hand over every piece of material you can find in your house. Take your socks off and walk over the bristly rug at your front door. Go squish your toes in the mud, as you did as a child. Sit and really *listen* to the city sounds outside. Take in the news and allow your emotions to be truly engaged by the terrible, happy, boring, heart-sobbing stories. Then turn the radio off and sit with those emotions a while. Go to the fridge and taste an olive. But really taste it. Let it fill your mind. Then take notes. What is this experience? What does it bring to mind? What memory does it elicit? What else is it like? Where does this smell take you? Allow the experience to inspire you. Allow the world to fully engage you, so you can fully engage your reader.

ASK THE OLD LADY IN THE CHECKOUT LINE ABOUT HER SHOES

Gail Anderson-Dargatz

Most fiction writers consider research a fundamental part of the writing process, but I'm constantly surprised by how few fiction writers conduct interviews for their fiction. My writing is often highly autobiographical or based on the stories of people I'm close to, and yet, for each project, I conduct a great many interviews with strangers or acquaintances. The reason? I want to push my story past the personal and into the universal, to gain inspiration for characters, situations, scenes, and plotlines. I want insight into patterns of behavior—how people generally respond to a given situation—and I want to seek out and get past my own personal biases and prejudices, to see my own story in a new light.

Lastly, I want to find those terrific details that lend authority to a scene. For example, as I was writing my upcoming novel, which takes place during the Salmon Arm fire of 1998, I did a pile of interviews with people who had lived through what until that time had been the largest peacetime evacuation in BC history. One man was on his roof setting up sprinklers on the day the firestorm swept through the valley. Fire was literally raining from the sky in the form of burning pinecones and needles. These bits landed on his arms, leaving welts the size of dimes and quarters, but he only noticed these burns later in the day. At the time, in the crisis of the moment, he swatted the burning debris away as if it were only mosquitoes that pestered him. You won't find that kind of detail in a book on forest fires.

If you find yourself hesitant about interviewing, consider that most people are dying to tell their stories, and if you are considerate and nonjudgmental in your approach, most will open up to you. What I do is explain a little of the fiction process to the people I interview, saying that undoubtedly the story will be transformed within my fiction, and that I will be writing from my own perspective, which will definitely be different from their own. People usually understand and are happy to be involved in this small way. Having said that, I still get the occasional letter from someone saying, "That's not the way it happened!" Expect that. We all remember things differently and, again, fiction will and should transform any story. Besides, when we read a book, we take our own imaginations, life histories, and expectations into the book with us, in effect creating the novel right along with the author. So each person who picks up the book will see it differently anyway.

▪▪▪ THE EXERCISE ▪▪▪▪▪▪▪▪▪▪▪▪▪▪▪▪▪▪▪▪▪▪▪▪▪▪▪▪▪▪▪▪

To find interview subjects, simply ask around. Ask a friend, co-worker, your honey, the guy sitting next to you on the bus if he knows of anyone who's had a similar experience to the one you're writing about, and listen to the stories that come your way. Look for commonalities, but look for differences as well. And above all, collect details. You'll find very quickly that there are patterns in all these stories. We are all humans. There are only so many ways that we respond to a given situation. At the same time, the details of the individual stories vary widely, and it's these details that will add texture and depth to your story.

In this process of research, you'll find that your own biases start to dissolve. Especially when working from personal stories, this needs to be your goal as a writer: to move past your own prejudices, your own assumptions, your own grip on how things were. It's very hard, and you won't be completely successful, but in the process of trying, you'll become a better writer. You'll also find yourself rethinking that personal story that started the fiction. You'll start gathering details from these other sources and rethinking scenes and characters; plots will change and grow. And as a result, your fiction will blossom.

INTERVIEW
T.C. Boyle

How do you get rolling at the writing desk?

After pacing round the house four hundred times, washing the walls, and licking the kitchen floor clean, after reading the *LA Times* and the *Santa Barbara News-Press* through, word by word, I find myself, unavoidably, at my desk. And there before me is the story/novel I was working on at this very desk just the day before. I am always astonished at the coincidence. I then reread what I've written, making small adjustments here and there, until I am in the land of the unseeing and unhearing, where, if I am lucky, the characters, themes, and language that comprise the story will continue to reveal themselves. If I am unlucky, I pace some more, re-lick the floor, etc.

How important to you is the first sentence of a story?

Of supreme importance. This is the magic portal, the way in which the writer—and the reader—can enter into a new, unfolding world. My favorite opening line is from one of my early stories, "Descent of Man." It goes like this: "I was living with a woman who suddenly began to stink."

What do you expect the first pages of a story to accomplish?

To insert the barbed hook into the reader's jaw. And to set said hook until the reader, flapping and gasping, is landed and netted, gutted, filleted, and fried.

How much foreknowledge of the story do you have at the beginning? Do you plot stories out in advance of writing them?

None whatever. Plot must come, like everything else, from the process of writing. All my work is organic, beginning with a vision and that first line and then following it to wherever it might go. Of course, along the way, I begin to discern just what that destination might be, but that is a day-to-day process of discovery.

What would you like to say on the subject of rewriting?

I rewrite constantly as I creep forward. But once the piece is set, that's it. I move on.

How do you approach research?

In the way that most of us, at one time or another, approached the dreaded term paper. I read deeply in a subject, compile notes (and sometimes, as in the case of *East Is East,* set in Georgia, or *Drop City,* set in Alaska, pay a visit to the locale), brood deeply, reread the notes obsessively, and wait in tension and misery and the prospect of failure, loss of talent and affect, for that magical first line to appear. In the case of *Drop City,* it came to me in this form: "The morning was a fish in a net, glistening and wriggling at the dead black border of her consciousness, but she'd never caught a fish in a net or on a hook either, so she couldn't really say if or how or why." This is the chemically altered consciousness of my main character, Star, who has recently arrived at Drop City to enjoy the brotherhood and sisterhood of the commune, and here she is on a sunny morning, tripping.

What did you give up in order to write?

Nothing whatever, if you discount the great opportunity of sticking with my band and becoming a wasted drone onstage in some third-rate club forever.

What's the hardest part of writing?

The middle.

What's the best part of writing?

The end.

THE TICKING CLOCK

Ron Carlson

The Ticking Clock exercise is simply an instrument to help a writer unify a narrative—and possibly find the second story he or she is attempting to write. A writer starts with a "timed" event and writes that episode(s) as completely and closely as he or she can, staying open to every possible side trip which is suggested in the day's work. I started using it to get my students to write stories that had greater coherence. The ticking clock event unifies the narrative and offers a framework in which the other story, the inner story, can live. So many times the inner story is revealed in flashbacks. The exercise illuminates a basic operating principle in much fiction: that we read to find out what happens while another story—sometimes deeper and more complicated and more subtle (and more focused on that thing called "character")—emerges. The outer story (the timed event) can be a quiet thing; it doesn't have to be some big-boned, thrilling cliffhanger.

▪▪▪ THE EXERCISE ▪▪▪▪▪▪▪▪▪▪▪▪▪▪▪▪▪▪▪▪▪▪▪▪▪▪▪▪▪▪▪▪▪▪▪

Write a short story of six hundred to a thousand words. The only criterion is that you establish a "ticking clock" in the first paragraph, something that must happen within a certain time period. Here are two student examples.

Example One

Proof
by W. Todd Kaneko

It was the year that Smokey Robinson played the Washington State Fair—my father was about to leave Seattle for good, although I didn't know it at the time. When he asked my mother if we might all go to the fair together, she said I could go if he promised to have me back by six that night so I could study for my algebra test the next day. She refused to go, however, insisting that there was good reason behind my parents' separation the previous year. He was irresponsible, she said. Immature and careless.

So my father brought Cyndi, a tall, platinum blond dressed in denim cutoffs, a bright pink tube-top and a California suntan. She was the receptionist at the transmission shop where my father worked and had only recently started hanging around with him. On the drive to Puyallup, she sat sideways in the front seat of his '86 Buick, her back against the passenger door. "What grade you in again, sugar?" she said, popping her gum.

"The boy's in eighth grade," my father said.

I told her I had just started ninth grade, and she giggled. She said I was cute and explained how she listened to Lynyrd Skynyrd when she was my age—she never dreamed that she would be going to see Smokey Robinson and the Miracles.

"It's just Smokey Robinson now," my father said.

"What happened to the Miracles?" Cyndi said.

My father shrugged and paid a lady five bucks to park on her lawn. We walked through the fair, my father and Cyndi several paces ahead of me as I kicked at the sawdust on the ground. The sugary aroma of Cracker Jacks and cotton candy mingled with the sharp odor of live-stock. We saw several breeds of chickens and a squash that weighed nearly two hundred pounds. At the dairy exhibit, Cyndi talked nonstop about the cows, even though she knew nothing except for what she read from the displays. She wouldn't ride any of the rides with us, but she watched as my father and I white-knuckled our way through the Tilt-a-Whirl, the Scrambler, and the Gravitron. In the Maze of Mirrors, my father swore every time he walked face first into a dead end, and on the way out he failed to notice how his lanky body was squished into the shape of a dwarf with a humongous head. We had a good time overall, but after the Dragon Swing, my father wrapped his arm around Cyndi's waist and kissed her on the mouth. She didn't seem surprised. I looked at my watch. "It's five," I said.

"What time does the show start?" she said.

"Smokey plays in an hour," my father said.

"I have to be back by six," I said.

My father looked at me like I was speaking a different language.

"I have an algebra test," I said.

He looked at Cyndi and then at me. "We came to see Smokey Robinson."

"I have to be back on time," I said. "Mom said—"

"I know what she said." My father ran his fingers through his hair and looked at the ground. "What the hell are you going to do with algebra anyways?" Cyndi popped her gum. "That's what they invented calculators for, right?"

"We're eating," he said, pulling a wad of bills out of his pocket. "Then it's Smokey Robinson, here we come."

Except for a belch from my father as we finished our cheeseburgers, we were silent as we ate. I thought of all the variables involved in repairing my parents' broken relationship. My father's indifference. My mother's stubborn will. Cyndi's stupidity. I figured that if my father got me home on time, my mother might take it as evidence that we might be able to exist as a family. I needed him to get us home.

"Cheer up," my father said when we got to the show. From where we stood in the middle of the small stadium, I could barely see through the crowd to the stage. If I was waiting for Ozzy Osbourne or Nirvana, I might have elbowed my way forward, but it all seemed pointless as we waited for Smokey Robinson to appear while the sun began its descent behind us.

"It's six-thirty," I said.

"Enough," he said. "She'll get over it."

Before I could reply, the stadium erupted into cheers and the music started—a gentle groove weaving its way through the crowd, coaxing couples to stand close and sway with the music. I didn't know any of the songs—they all sounded kind of the same to me. And as Smokey neared the end of his set, my father whacked me in the arm.

"This is a good song," my father said. "Remember this song. Tell your mother about it." My father stood with his eyes pointed stageward, but he was focused someplace else. Smokey Robinson sang about loving and leaving; he sang about a love so strong it drives people apart—and when Smokey went into the chorus of "You've Really Got a Hold on Me," my father coughed several times into his hand. Cyndi placed her chin on his shoulder but he stepped away from her, putting me between them. He placed his heavy palms on my shoulders and squeezed, his nails black with grime from the shop. "Remember," he breathed.

But I didn't tell my mother about the song. After dropping Cyndi off, we got home around ten-thirty. My parents argued about duty and respect for about twenty minutes before my father finally slammed the front door. I passed my algebra test the next day but just barely. My father moved away to Detroit a month later. He unfailingly sent my mother child support until my eighteenth birthday, when he sent me a card along with a check for five hundred dollars, which I still haven't cashed.

Ron Carlson: What surprised you in writing this exercise? What did you find out in the writing?

W. Todd Kaneko: When I started *Proof*, I had two characters, a song, and a ticking clock: Get home on time or else. I chose the state fair as a setting because it seemed like the kind of thing boys do with their fathers. I had trouble figuring out the clock's value in the piece, so I let it be and trusted that it would work itself out as I felt my way through the story. I thought I was working toward an epiphanic moment in the funhouse as the boy recognizes a distorted image of his father, but the story shifted when I found Cyndi, whose presence helped focus the value of the family, redefined the value of the clock, and complicated the agendas of both father and son. Her existence necessitated a penultimate moment between all three, and I was pleasantly surprised to arrive at the concert at the story's end.

Example Two

The Scooter
by Elizabeth Weld

She told me it was a nice day and, if I wanted, I could go outside. "Be back here at four," she said. "Or ten 'till. I don't want to go looking."

Dr. Wagner was standing in the hall by the water fountain with her pad on her hip. I always wondered if she had kids, but then I'd forget to tell my mom to ask her.

I said, "I'll be back at four. You always get out at ten after."

She looked at me. "I don't want to argue," she said.

I had a *Highlights* magazine in my lap, which now looked stupid, so I put it back and stood up. My mom stood up and followed Dr. Wagner. There was no one in the office except for me and the receptionist, who was bent over her computer. I tried to leave with the air of someone older than ten. I stepped outside and pulled the door closed behind me.

Outside there were birds chirping and two cars drove by and a plane was dragging its contrail toward the horizon. It wasn't hot for May. It was the first day of summer vacation. Next to me, the olive trees had ruined the sidewalk. I walked the other direction toward the highway. Two doors down, I found a boy in his driveway bent over a scooter. All around him, tools lay in the dirt. A red plastic container of gasoline sat near him, and this attracted me. I wouldn't have stopped, but I honestly dropped my keys, and when I crouched down, he and I were eye level.

"Do you know what time it is?" he said.

"A little after three," I said.

"Dang." He stood up wiped his hands on his jeans. I wiped my hands on my thighs too.

"How old are you?" he said. He was standing up, watching me. He had orange hair and clear, tan skin that didn't fit with his hair.

"Is that your real hair?" I said.

He stuck his hand in his hair and pulled it up and let it go and most of it stayed up. "What are you talking about?" he said.

"I'm ten," I said.

He said, "I'm eleven."

I pointed at the scooter, which was altered and elaborate. "Is that yours?"

He said, "I'm building it for my baby brother. He can't walk."

I stepped closer. He gestured. It looked like a scooter, but the part where you stood had been widened. And there was a motor.

"He's not a baby," he said, "but he can't walk." He patted the handle affectionately. "I'm going to drive him around the neighborhood."

"Did your dad help you make this?" I said.

"He helps at night," he said.

I looked at the street. It was probably 3:20. I was guessing, being conservative. "You know where my mom is?"

He shook his head.

I said, "Therapy." He looked at me, but I held my ground. I wanted to go ahead and get it out, so he could decide if he wanted to be friends.

He looked up the street toward the clinic. He seemed unconcerned. He turned around and lifted the widened seat, and I saw that it hadn't been attached to the scooter.

"I'd give you a ride," he said, "but it's not safe yet. This thing falls off."

When I crouched down next to him, he touched the wheel and said, "My brother can't talk either. He drools. He's handicapped. If he comes out, don't make fun of him."

I could tell right away that most of the work had been done by his father. His tools consisted mainly of bungee cords and tape and scissors. He didn't seem to know much more than me. We tried some things that didn't work, which took a while. It was fun; he held the tape and I held the scissors. Then we traded. But our real breakthrough came when we stopped being conservative with the duct tape. We just started wrapping the platform over and over, over the platform, under the scooter, the way soccer players wrap their cleats with their laces. Once it was firmly attached, he stepped back and frowned.

"I wanted it to be wooden," he said. "It's ugly."

He was right. It looked like the pipes in our attic.

I said, "Paint it."

"It won't look good," he said.

"Fine," I said. "Unwrap the whole thing and wait for your dad to come back and fix it for you."

"I'm just saying," he said.

"My mom's getting out any minute," I said. "I wanted to ride on it."

"What happens if you're late?"

"She gets frustrated."

"Is she crazy?"

"No." I kicked the cardboard duct tape core and it flew further than I had expected. "It's clinical depression."

I could tell he wasn't impressed. I sighed, to change the subject, and said, "I wanted to ride on this, but now I don't have time."

He said, "I'll give you a ride back to her then. What's your name?"

I'd forgotten that he didn't know. I said, "Jenny."

He said, "I'm David."

I said, "We have to hurry."

"You'll get there quicker this way," he said. "So you'll probably be on time."

He opened the gas and I opened the gas cap on the motor and he poured, carefully, breathing through his teeth. I listened to him breathing. The gas smelled wonderful. When he pulled the cord, the thing started right away. I was feeling a little desperate, because in truth, my mother did get angry. A real quiet, lonely-making angry, and then she'd go to her room and sleep. This would last through dinner, which would be me eating fish sticks alone in the kitchen. Later she'd come down and say that I had frightened her. I'd apologize and go to bed planning to never be late again.

While he pushed the scooter onto the street I looked straight up, because I was anxious and it's something I do, a little like praying, and the sun got right in my eyes. I sneezed and he pushed a red button and said, "That's the choke."

He angled the scooter toward Dr. Wagner's office and stepped on, and after a second, I stepped on behind him. We both stood there for a second, then I put my hands on his shoulders. His shoulders were warm. Once I did this, he made the scooter go forward.

It was very slow. It went about a quarter of the speed of walking. We rode for a few seconds, then he stopped and stepped off. I stayed on and watched him.

"Maybe you're too heavy," he said.

"You're heavier than I am," I said.

"But my little brother is a lot lighter than you," he said.

I stepped off, offended. We were both disappointed.

He got back on and tried it, and the thing went just as slowly.

"A blip," he said, a term I guessed was his father's. "Dad'll recalibrate."

I nodded. Now I was late and had no reason, and loneliness stretched out before me like an ultimately familiar horizon. I hated fish sticks. I hated tarter sauce. And to be honest, I hated summer vacation. No one ever came over to our house. My mother napped.

I sat around listening to the air-conditioning click on and off, looking at the patterns I'd made pacing around on the carpet.

"David, I was supposed to be back," I said.

He looked at me when I said his name. "Okay," he said. "We could push it. We'll get back on right in front of the office."

Relief filled my chest like cool water. But as soon as we started walking, I began to see that what we were doing wasn't logical. It wasn't getting us there any faster. The sidewalk in front of us didn't seem to move closer, and finally I couldn't bear it.

"I'm going to run," I said. "I'll bring her out to see you."

I ran and felt the glory of my body on the road while my mind made up explanations for my mother. "I met a boy with a handicapped brother." "I'm building something." "I'm sorry."

When I got to the front of the building, she was standing with one hand on her purse, her other hand tracing something in the cement wall beside her. When she saw me she straightened her skirt. I stopped running, then started again. Before she could talk, I started, looking down so her face wouldn't stop me.

"I met a boy," I said. "I didn't mean to be late, but we built a scooter for his brother and we wanted to finish so we could show you."

I looked up and she was peering at me. I rushed backward into the street. "Will you come look?" I said. "Please?" I was acting blindly now, living out my last freedom in a panic.

She stepped out onto the soiled sidewalk and picked her way through the fallen olives. David was still about twenty feet away, coming along very slowly. "Wave, Mom," I said.

She waved. David lifted one hand and smiled uncertainly and looked back down. Suddenly, it looked so bizarre that I lost my steam. She could sense this and took her opportunity.

"Jenny," she said.

"I'm sorry," I said.

She said, "I thought maybe you might come with me next week, to talk to Dr. Wagner."

"I didn't even know what time it was," I said. "You didn't give me the phone."

She looked at David. She said, "Dr. Wagner thinks I'm not letting you be a kid. She thinks you might be having a hard time being a child."

I said, "We built this thing to carry his handicapped brother. He can't walk, and he's going to drive him around the neighborhood. Isn't that a good cause?"

When I looked up, she had tears in her eyes. But now he was here.

"This is David," I said.

He said hi. He looked at my mom and then back at me. My mother said hello. I don't think it was obvious that she was crying. I wished she would say something nice about his scooter, but I knew she wouldn't, not out of meanness, but just because it wasn't on her mind.

"Jenny was helping me," he said.

"I'll be back next week," I said.

"My dad'll have it fixed by then," he said.

I said, "We could paint it."

"Right." He turned it and stepped on and motored away, slowly. My mom was already walking toward the car. The sun was turning into the evening sun, which I hated.

When we got in the car, she put it in reverse and told me to put on my seatbelt.

"I didn't mean to make you mad," I said.

"I'm not mad," she said, but her face was pinched and white. She said, "That's not what it is."

I said, "If you want, we could eat in your room. I could bring you dinner."

We didn't listen to the radio, which is okay, because the radio fills the car. When I'm alone in the quiet I have huge thoughts. That's one advantage to the quiet. No other kid my age is having thoughts like mine. Alone in the silence, with no one to bother you. Time stopping thoughts. Thoughts that make you nauseous.

"Did you like making that scooter?" my mother said.

"Yeah."

"Do you think I let you be a child? A normal child?"

I said, "Mom, you're good. I feel like a child. I have no responsibilities."

"That's true," she said, her shoulders relaxing. "We should get you some chores."

I sat back and kicked my feet and looked out the window. There weren't any other cars. I wanted to tell her I didn't want to eat dinner by myself anymore, that for some reason it frightened me.

"David's brother can't talk," I said. "He's not a baby either. He's just handicapped. He drools."

"That's sad," she said.

I nodded. "It's a tragedy."

She turned to me. When she smiled, I knew that it was true, that she was a good mother. My heart filled with glory. The glory pressed upward in my chest until I couldn't breathe and I looked at my mother. She wasn't looking at me, but I was sure she felt it too.

Ron Carlson: What surprised you in the writing of this exercise?

Elizabeth Weld: I decided to make my ticking clock the hour that a girl's mother spends in therapy. This immediately caused a problem because I had a character with an hour to spend and nothing to do. She was bored. So my first surprise was David, who was helpful because he had a project. Everything after that was unplanned and caused by problem-solving. I was surprised that even though I couldn't pause to describe things or meander—everything had to move the story forward—the story didn't go where I expected. I wanted the last scene to be David and Jenny flying along on the scooter. They felt a lot of urgency and I wanted to relieve them of it before the story ended. I thought I would do this by fixing the scooter, but it turned out that what they needed was friendship.

SUGGESTED READING

Some stories to consider: "The Horse Dealer's Daughter" by D.H. Lawrence; "Cross Country Snow" by Ernest Hemingway; "Save the Reaper" by Alice Munro; "Old Boys, Old Girls" by Edward P. Jones.

LEARNING TO BE A NOTEBOOK NERD

Andrew Pyper

One need not be a writer to have had the experience of being struck by a great idea while in the middle of something—soaping armpits in the shower, driving home from work, pushing a cart through supermarket aisles—and, moments later, finding the idea has disappeared. *Poof.* A creative lightning bolt, the resolution to an internal debate, a recollected bit of juicy gossip. Now gone. Never to return.

For writers, of course, the problem of losing one's best ideas has even more serious consequences. Ideas, both big and small (and, let's face it, most of the time, they're on the small side), are what we trade in. We can't afford to let them slip out the brain's back door without at least leaving a trace behind. This is why one of the habits that resourceful writers develop is being a notebook nerd.

Carrying around a back-pocket notepad may be something of an inconvenience, and nobody's saying that a pen clipped to your shirt collar is a cool fashion accessory. In addition, you can expect raised eyebrows of suspicion ("Are you a cop or something?") and sympathetic, he's-obviously-unwell looks from passersby when you stop on the street to scratch something down.

On the bright side, the advantages of being a notebook nerd are numerous. Not only do you capture the Eureka! ideas that may visit, but bringing a notebook with you wherever you go assists not only in seeing and hearing and smelling the world but in recording these impressions as they occur. In short, being a notebook nerd helps one *think* like a writer at all times, instead of only when sitting at the desk, when the world can often seem distant and difficult to summon in all of its sensual particulars.

■■■ THE EXERCISE ■■■■■■■■■■■■■■■■■■■■■■■■■■■■■■■■■

Purchase the smallest notepad you can find, and the pen least likely to bleed ink through your clothes. Find the most handy places on your person—knapsack, purse, pocket, tied around your neck—to keep these tools. Then go about your normal business, but now with a commitment to never trust that you will remember that funny thing you saw someone wearing, the interesting way a three-legged dog gets around, the smell from the pizza place around the corner, or the curious conversation between two strangers on the subway. Write it down. There, on the spot. Bite into life as it comes fresh and hot out of the oven. Then, later, at the writing desk, you can call upon your catalog of notes to enhance your physical descriptions or characterizations or dialogue or scene settings and give them the unique detailing that makes them real (because they *are* real).

If you have trouble discerning between the "good stuff" that is worthy of being written down and the dull chaff of everyday life, know that everything—at least potentially, if given sufficient attention—is good stuff.

In order to help you get into the notebook nerd habit, here are some exercises that are guaranteed to produce some surprising bits and pieces that can make your writing projects gain a more organic, idiosyncratic veracity.

1. **Go to a public place where you are in close quarters with others.** A bar, the streetcar, the food court. Tune into an ongoing conversation between two or more people next to you and, without any adornment, record what they say to each other. Be totally objective: Don't correct slang or mispronunciations or interruptions. Be a human tape recorder.

2. **Walk along the street and take note of isolated aspects of people as they pass.** How they walk, for instance. How long they wear their trousers. Do they meet eyes with others as they pass or stare at their own feet? Become aware of the infinite distinctions that exist within any anonymous group.

3. **Smell.** By far, this is the sense that is overlooked in most writing, and the one that, if described well, can deliver the reader directly into a scene. Move through a day of your life taking note of its palette of odors.

4. **Notes to self.** Outside of your normal work area, think about the writing project you are currently working on. Consider different ways to order events, why a character does a certain thing, how you think the story should end. Make note of any solutions that come to mind. Sometimes, being physically away from the office can give rise to great ideas—but without your notebook, they'll be gone by the time you return to the desk.

SUGGESTED READING

Russell Smith is a friend of mine, one whose writing I admire. It is because of this friendship that I know that he is a notebook nerd. His pitch-perfect, hilarious dialogue proves it. Russell will often eat dinner on his own and scribble down whatever people are saying around him, noting how our speech communicates our class, pretensions, attractions, and insecurities in addition to whatever it is that we meant to say.

Russell is the author of three very funny, satirical novels, but perhaps the best works in which to observe his dialogue are the short stories collected in *Young Men*.

Advice

Writing is not an activity limited to the time you work the keyboard or scribble on the page but how you process the world during all your waking—and dreaming—hours. Opportunities for great lines or original stories fly past us all the time, but only real writers are able to recognize them for what they are and capture them before they escape. Thinking like a writer, then, is a mode of consciousness where everything is translatable into the grand narrative of our experience.

FIVE TIPS

Margot Livesey

1. Alone at our desks we often forget how rich and varied life is. Spend an hour in a public place—café, library, park, shop—and study the people around you. Note how many gestures, expressions, and details are ones you seldom see in stories and maybe don't know quite how to describe. People do far more than nod, shrug, smile, and frown. Try to find ways to describe what you're actually seeing.

2. Take a scene in a story. First strip out all obvious references to emotion. Would a reader know what the emotions are? How could you make the reader more fully aware of the unspoken emotions?

3. We are often our own most zealous censors. Take a scene in a story. Overwrite madly. Indulge in purple prose, wild metaphors, lush descriptions, excess of all kinds. With luck you'll find some new ways to describe emotions.

4. Sometimes what we won't do is just as central as what we do do. Describe a character in terms of all the things she or he would never do. She would never eat a mushroom gathered

by a friend, use chopsticks in a Chinese restaurant, sing "Happy Birthday," pat a strange dog... Allow your character to do one thing you would never do.

5. Often our scenes are not very dramatic because we are treating our non-point-of-view characters as second class citizens, forcing them to do whatever is needed to allow the point-of-view character to have his or her say. Rewrite a scene from the point of view of a non-point-of-view character. How does your perception of the scene and the main character change?

INTERVIEW
Michael Redhill

What is your process for writing a short story versus writing a novel? How do they differ for you, and how are they similar?

A novel is a long-term consideration that benefits, in my case, from lengthy periods of percolation. I like to work concertedly on a novel, then leave it alone for a while before coming back to it. When I write short fiction, I try to get through a complete draft quickly in order to maintain the compressed impression that is usually its seed. Short fiction comes to me as gestures that need fleshing out; it's a little tidy to say that a novel is the opposite, but it's at least a little true: a novel comes to me needing its gestures, while the overall mood or flavor of the novel form is often unchanged from its original inspiration by the time I get to the end of it. A short story is a room, a novel a house. What they have in common is the requirement of intensive renovation—nothing I write is close to finished by the time I get through a first draft. I also think I'm attracted to issues of character and relationship when I write short fiction, but for me, the novel is an attempt to understand and express some aspect of the world. The characters and their relationships are obviously important, but larger considerations tend to shape them in novels.

What do you expect the first pages of a story to accomplish?

As a reader and writer of short fiction, I have the same expectations/hopes of the opening of a short story: I want to feel I'm in the presence of a strong voice.

I want the emotions and the storytelling to grab me immediately. I have little patience with a short story—I expect in a form as compacted as short fiction that something is going to burst off the page and grab me around the throat. It doesn't have to be on the level of plot, however; it can be the fierce originality of the writing, the voice. I've read fewer successful short stories than I've read successful novels. I think the challenge of short fiction is underrated—the idea that short story collections are some kind of apprenticeship to the novel strikes me as the same as suggesting a doctor should learn brain surgery in order to understand the body entire.

Describe the editorial work you do. How does it impact your fiction writing? Poetry?

I do a couple different kinds of editorial work. I teach workshops at the university level, but I also do close editing on authors who care for my particular style of reading, as well as authors who are going to be published in *Brick,* a magazine I publish and edit for. At the university level, I read with an eye to helping younger writers see what is and what isn't working in the prose sentence or the poetic line. I try my best to read for intent so that I can address writing issues on the level of what it *appears* the author is trying to do. It can get more prescriptive when I'm editing for the magazine, however, where it's expected that I, as a publisher, may ask for certain things that are not present, in order to serve my readers, who come first in this instance. When I'm editing friends, I just try to jump in with both feet and offer the kind of comprehensive commentary that I know I need when I'm ready for readers. Anything can help, so I open my mind and say what comes into it. The way this affects my own writing is hard to measure—editing is central to my experience as both a reader and a writer— the possibility of improvement is always alive in my world, so I don't think of my editorial voice as affecting my writing one way or the other: it's an important part of it all.

Do new writers have the same editorial experience with publishers as writers twenty years ago had? Do they now have to emerge fully formed, as it were?

This is an excellent question. I doubt that professional editors today are as thoroughly educated and well-read as the editors of one or two generations ago. There's a certain amount of textual dramaturgy that passes for editing these days, and although I've been lucky in the editors I've been associated with, the number of clearly under-edited books that appear these days is testament to editing being a lost art. The frenzy to find the next big thing is a part of this—first novels have enormous cachet these days, and I think they're rushed to market at the expense of the authors. One thing I tell writing students is that there's no boat to miss when it comes to publishing: there is always the next season. The only thing you can do wrong is to publish before you're ready. Once it's out there, you don't get to take it back.

How important are literary journals for new writers?

Literary journals are of huge importance because they're the open mics of the publishing world. By cutting one's teeth in small magazines, writers are joining a community that is interested in what newer writers have to say. I find the world of literary journals vibrant and engaged, and I think it's a pity when newer writers disdain the riches they offer. At some important level, the only truly useful discourse around literary publishing is happening at this level because small magazines are not driven by the need to make a profit. Small magazines publish out of love and commitment, and what they offer readers and writers alike is an unalloyed experience of experimentation.

What is the current thinking about simultaneous submissions?

I think as long as you're being honest and straightforward with magazines or publishers, simultaneous submissions are fine. Some have a policy against it, however, so it's best to look into it before you send multiples.

When you read books as a writer—what are you looking for and how do you use reading to inform your own writing?

I'm fascinated by how good writing works, and so I read to learn and absorb as much as I read for pleasure or for information. I'd rather read a brilliantly written book about something dull than have the opposite experience. I'm a sentence snob: I find it very hard trekking to get through a poorly written book. I remember encountering Bruce Chatwin for the first time, in his book *The Songlines,* and thinking that I doubted I'd really be able to get into it because of the subject matter, but I was riveted by it. I could read Chatwin's phone messages and be engaged by them. It comes down to that hard-to-define quantity that we call "voice" because we don't know what else to call it, but great writing has a personality all of its own, and that's what attracts me to a book more than anything else: the quality of its personality. I read widely, and I try to read deeply, and as long as the author is giving me a reason to pay attention, I'll listen for as long as they care to talk.

How do you approach research?

I love research, and not only because of the procrastinatory opportunities it presents. I find that research puts me into my right brain and, by working on fiction in this parallel fashion (I'm in the world of my work, but I'm not actually writing), it opens up new and unexpected vistas for me. Research often suggests answers to problems I didn't realize I had yet. In my most recent novel, *Consolation,* an 1850s pharmaceutical formulary gave me smells and tastes and physical realities I hadn't even considered, and gave life to aspects of the book in a way I could never have predicted. I research widely, sometimes even randomly, with an open mind.

What is the biggest challenge for you technically with your fiction writing?

I'm never satisfied with the quality of my sentences. I can hew them to the best shape possible for me, but I know they can be better. When I read my published work, I often sweat the lost opportunities. I also find that I get bogged down in stage management in my plotting—I get obsessed with people entering and exiting rooms, which way they're facing, what their hands are doing, and I think sometimes this has the effect of making scenes that could be more dramatic too static. I'm aware of these problems (and too many other, smaller, embarrassing ones I'm not willing to cop to here), and so I write conscious of them. Suffice it to say the shape of what I'm thinking about is not the thing that ends up on the page. The transmutation that happens between the mind and the keyboard is acted upon by some kind of spiritual chemical I still don't have control of.

What skills does a new writer need in order to be published and connect with readers?

Patience and detachment. Patience because rushing to print, as I've said, is a huge mistake, and there are those who are willing to abet a younger writer's urge to be published. Standing back and recognizing that every gesture of a writing life is part of a larger action can help an inexperienced writer to restrain the kinds of ego needs that lead to putting something out in the world before it's ready. And detachment is probably even more important: unless you're deliberately writing for a certain kind of audience, you can't expect to be rewarded for putting down on paper what was in your heart. Generally, the world doesn't care about your heart, and hoping for approval (never mind adulation) is a fast-track to losing the small, hot thing that made you want to write in the first place. Celebrity, awards, supposed achievement: all these things are illusory. I wish a book well when it goes out into the world, and then thank god that I've got something new to work on. Being read, being understood, being loved—should any of this come your way, it should be considered cream. Those who write for these things sooner or later become false to themselves. The only true joy, and the only true achievement, is the work.

WRITING AS RE-ENACTION

Steven Heighton

There is a technique that's at the very heart of literary fiction, yet it's never mentioned in book reviews or at book club meetings, and hardly ever discussed even in academic criticism or during writing seminars. In those forums people tend to discuss things like writers' themes, their voices, their socioeconomic backgrounds, their characters and whether or not those characters are entirely lovable. But a book is built out of words. As Paul Fussell wrote about Evelyn Waugh, "[He] knew that writing is an affair of words rather than soul, impulse, 'sincerity,' or an instinct for the significant. If the words aren't there, nothing happens." And as Don DeLillo once said of Hemingway and his distinctive habit of linking a series of unpunctuated clauses with the word *and:* "[That one] word is more important to Hemingway's work than Africa or Paris."

Not that any of these writers would deny that "an instinct for the significant" is a staple trait for a good writer. But the point remains that good writing starts with words—words artfully arranged to create specific effects. Maybe we overlook this point because it seems too obvious; or because the effects, and the way the words create them, can be difficult to talk about; or because most of what we read, in newspapers, weekly magazines, manuals, self-help books, etc., is written in functional, utilitarian prose—prose designed to be transparent, a mere conveyance bringing us information or a message. Which is fine for that purpose. But in truly literary fiction, the writing is never just functional. Literary fiction uses a number of fascinating techniques—essentially the techniques of poetry, though generally deployed in a more subtle way—so that the writing actually embodies or becomes the thing it's about, acoustically *recreating* what it describes, the words in their artful patterns re-enacting the scene, image, or description so that the writing and what's written about are indissolubly fused. Form and content, welded together.

Here's a brief example from my own work. I make it Exhibit A simply because I know what I was trying to do with the sentence and thus can't be accused of reading too much into it. Our protagonist, Sevigne (Sev-EEN), is in a bar, feeling blue, as protagonists in bars are wont to do; deciding to leave, he stands and abruptly notices that he's drunk. He makes his way downstairs to street level in the following line: *Sevigne, suddenly drunk, stumbles down the stairs to the door.* What I wanted was for that sentence to give an impression of stumbling—for the words themselves to be stumbling downward, too fast, tripping over the close-paired commas and the hard staccato *d* sounds in "suddenly" and "drunk." And then there's the repetitive onomatopoeic sibilance—like a drunken slurring—of the four alliterative *s* words. And the way the sentence clunks to a landing at street level on its last short syllable, and on a third hard *d*: *door*. I wanted the reader not only to *see* Sevigne stumbling downstairs but to experience the stumble from within his point of view—the sentence re-enacting the numb blur and accelerated temporality of intoxication.

Ideally, readers won't notice any of this on a conscious level. Ideally, it just makes the action more vivid, so readers feel that they're sensually *present* in the text in a way they would not be if, say, a character's drunken departure were rendered in a less orchestrated, more reportorial way. And the purpose of all this fuss? Simply to ensure maximum vitality. To ensure that the words and the story "stay read" (as Merilyn Simonds puts it). It's no easy job, because the words themselves, when flickering on a screen or printed on a page, are mere signs, lifeless abstractions. A writer tries to breathe life into them by arranging them so as to create a simulacrum of life—to make the reader feel what the writer felt upon seeing or imagining the thing described. And writers have to use every trick at their disposal because they stand at several removes from the reader. They can't leap across that divide with dazzling slashes of color like a painter, giant images and Dolby sound like a filmmaker, the heart-stalling kettle-drum roll of a composer. All they have is language, which, as we all know, divides us as much as it connects us. Words are a modest medium.

Still, this re-enactive writing has a fighting chance of bridging the wide synapse between writer and reader because it not only speaks to the mind but affects the senses. It has been shown that the heart rate of someone listening to music accelerates or slows down in accord with the beat of the music. The heart, in a sense, is trying to entrain with the beat, in the same ways a fetus's heart entrains with its mother's. The rhythms of good prose can have a similar effect on a reader, drawing the body as well as the brain into the reading experience. And though I don't have neurological/physiological proof at my fingertips, I'm prepared to believe that something experienced in sensual as well as cerebral terms will be more affecting and stay in the memory longer than, say, a piece of writing that induces a purely mental response.

I've explained the mechanics of that stumbling sentence of my own. Now here's an example from classic literature: James Joyce's *Ulysses*. It's an evocation of the night sky as seen above a Dublin yard, if I'm remembering right, by Leopold Bloom and Stephen Dedalus: *Heaventree hung with humid nightblue fruit.*

This textual moment occurs at one of those points where the writing in a prose work aspires to the condition of poetry, and achieves it, in order to make an especially important scene or image leap to special clarity. Here Joyce *shows* us the stars by using alliteration—the three *h*'s in *heaventree, hung,* and *humid*—along with the strong assonance of the repeated hard-*u* sounds in *humid, blue,* and *fruit*—to achieve a kind of verbal pointillism. The accelerating stress pattern of the line, which crowds three single, stressed syllables into the end of the sentence—*night*—*blue*—*fruit*—enhances the effect: a staccato of pointillist stars being poked into our consciousness. And finally, the cool sounds of those long *u*'s help suggest the blue coolness of the night sky.

▪▪▪ THE EXERCISE ▪▪▪▪▪▪▪▪▪▪▪▪▪▪▪▪▪▪▪▪▪▪▪▪▪▪▪▪▪▪▪▪▪▪▪▪

Write a sentence or two, or a full paragraph, in which the writing re-enacts or re-creates instead of just reporting or describing. It's easiest to apply re-enactive techniques to moments of physical action (though also easy to overdo it at such times—be aware). Some suggestions: a woman stumbling down the stairs of a bar among fleeing customers after a fire or a gunfight has erupted; a man bounding up a winding outdoor staircase on the way to see his beloved fiancée—or, maybe, on the way to break off the engagement; an animal of some kind, with its distinctive movements, crossing a park or peering through the bars of its cage at a zoo, etc.

This technique is not limited to physical drama, of course; it can be used effectively to re-embody the processes of thought, as Henry James did so complexly. So try re-creating the inner monologue of a man contemplating murder, or robbery, or an act of benevolent self-sacrifice, giving special attention to the rhythms of the writing, since those rhythms are the pulse rate of the prose—and, by association, of the character. Or concoct your own scene or moment.

SUGGESTED READING

All the great fiction writers use re-enactive techniques to a certain extent. Some do it more by instinct, others more by design. (Most, I think, do it by instinct in the first draft and then enhance the effects in the course of revision.) True esthetes like Joyce, Nabokov, Flaubert, and Guy Davenport seem to use the techniques self-consciously in every sentence; certainly the first few paragraphs of *Lolita* constitute a sort of free clinic in conspicuously re-enactive writing ("the tip of the tongue taking a trip of three steps down the palate to tap, at three, on the teeth"). Other great writers, like Mavis Gallant and Alice Munro, use the techniques more selectively, permitting themselves to use a more transparent, reportorial mode in some connective or expository passages. Still, the opening page of Munro's widely anthologized masterpiece "Royal Beatings" is an object lesson in verbal re-enaction. Malcolm Lowry's *Under the Volcano* is one of the best examples of sustained re-enactive writing, right down to the often turgid syntax and diction that simulates the garrulous mental and verbal meanderings of a drunk. And consider the structure of Lowry's backwardly revolving description of an ominous Ferris wheel: "Over the town, in the dark tempestuous night, backwards revolved the luminous wheel."

Advice

Interest is never enough. If it doesn't haunt you, you'll never write it well. What haunts and obsesses you into writing may, with luck and labor, interest your readers; what merely interests you is likely to bore them.

FIVE TIPS

Richard House

1. **Writing process.** Most writing manuals focus on the process of writing, of getting words onto paper or screen. Much of this you'll discover yourself. It can take a while, and it can change from project to project. Writing, for me, can be incremental, so I usually carry about a notebook. It's worth noting what time of the day you prefer to write (or concentrate best). Set a place to write, and establish some kind of routine—as much for yourself as for the other people in your life. If necessary, set limits about noise and interruptions. If seclusion is what you need, there are writer's residencies (or, if you can afford it, organize a break independently). It's a good way to focus, particularly at the start or close of a project, and you will meet like-minded people.

2. **Talk and read.** Discuss what you are working on—this is always useful. Explain what you are aiming for, or what you have done, and pay attention to how you re-figure what you are talking about. This can be dynamic, especially if you are speaking with someone who works in another creative field,

and remember to return the favor. Be aware that some people are poor listeners and butt in with wacky advice, or dismiss what you're trying to say, or automatically compare what you are doing with something that has already been done. Depending on what stage you are at, a bad discussion can wreck an idea that possibly had more or further possibility. It can be difficult to listen to a mess of ideas as they sort themselves out, but this can save you from hours of frustrated writing. Read your work out loud, to yourself, and at events (readings/performances); this helps when you tire of reading through the work on paper or screen.

3. **Schedule and deadlines.** If I'm finding it hard to focus, I have to set the day into blocks. When I follow this, I'm productive, even on a day I don't feel much like working. If I don't, things are generally a mess. Take into consideration if you are someone who works well with a deadline (steadily towards it), or crashes into them (up all night the day before). It helps to know temperamentally how you work, and to understand how much time something might take. Playing and manipulating words isn't always easy or productive, so don't be too harsh on yourself when you don't seem to be getting anywhere.

4. **Form and Audience.** Consider other options. It is possible that one larger project (a novel), might generate smaller pieces. It is also possible that what you are writing isn't a novel, a short story, a poem, or a screenplay, and you are spending too much time wrestling with the constraints of these forms. Language swims about us in conversation, on billboards, in music, on the worldwide web. Writers often assume or aim for a generic group (the reading public), which doesn't have to be the case. Thinking about who you

want to read your work might mean that a different form is more appropriate (something scratched on a table, whispered to one person, projected into the street, stitched onto a banner, spelled out in fire, tattooed onto your inner thigh). It is as laudable to write for one person as it is for many.

5. **Research.** There doesn't have to be a big difference between collecting and researching material, and writing. You don't have to do all the research first and then retire somewhere to write. Research (for me) covers conversations, reading, interviews, pursuing activities I wouldn't otherwise consider or make the opportunity for. An example: I worked with a collaborative public-art group for ten years. Each project was devised on-site, specifically for that place, and would be determined by what we discovered and who we met. In an attempt to map San Francisco, we decided to spend the working day (and in the event a couple of night shifts) with people working in the city. We started with one person who recommended someone else, and the piece grew naturally from there. We went with a helicopter journalist, a dive team who services the Bay Bridge (and recovers bodies from San Francisco Bay), an illegal worker, a wine merchant, and a baker. The final piece—a collection of sounds and recorded interviews—wasn't so hot, but the process of making the work made for some remarkable experiences. I've attempted to use this approach in my writing. One of the most interesting aspects of writing is having a life, being active and talking with people, experiencing stuff, any kind of stuff, learning about people and about the world in tiny, tiny fractions. Most people generally respect creative writers—credentials don't seem that necessary—and this opens doors. If you have

a notion of what you want to write lodged in your head, then much of what you do can feed into that, and hopefully, the reverse also happens, and the world begins to inform and change what you have to say.

WHAT'S YOUR MYTH?

Priscila Uppal

As Karen Armstrong tells us in *A Short History of Myth,* "Because the novelist and the artist are operating at the same level of consciousness as mythmakers, they naturally resort to the same themes." Mythology and storytelling used to be one and the same, and likely still are, though we sometimes like to separate them in modern times.

Myths, fables, and fairy tales are, usually, our first stories; and they hold a special place in our imaginations as a result. As a child, I could spend afternoons running around as picnic-basket-carrying Little Red Riding Hood or the abandoned child with breadcrumbs, Gretel. On rainy days, I would even play with my dolls, brush their hair and cut it off, as in Samson and Delilah. The morality of many of the tales, such as Abraham and Isaac, Rumpelstiltskin, or The Troll Under the Bridge, intrigued me, tormented me, astonished me, confused me—most of all caused me to ask questions about the world and my surroundings as I looked for correspondences between the stories I was told and the reality of my day-to-day life.

When I think of various family stories that have been told to me, and that remain with me, they frequently correspond to the plots or themes of desires of the myths, fables, or fairy tales of my childhood. For instance, my father and his brothers all immigrated to North America from India, and each concentrated on building both a career and family. I think of them like the Three Little Pigs, each trying to build the strongest, most durable house, out of the finest materials, so the Big Bad Wolf of life won't be able to huff and puff and blow it down (unfortunately, our house was made of straw).

When I am in the middle of writing a story, I sometimes ask myself, "What myth are you telling?" Although the answer might not be evident, inevitably I am able to draw upon the history of my reading and listening so that I can grasp my own story through the lens of archetypal myth, fable, or fairy tale. I can trace back my own short stories "Burning Pieces" and "Sleepwalking," for instance, to the classical Greek myths of Philomela and Medea, even though there are no direct references to mythology in the stories. The Philomela myth, in which a woman's tongue is cut out so that she cannot name her rapist, is a tale of trauma and the forceful silencing of truth; my own nameless narrator of "Burning Pieces" sets fires because she is unable to talk directly about her own childhood traumas. "Sleepwalking," although a story told from the point of view of a woman somnambulist's feet, is a story, like Medea, about love and betrayal, and the ways in which morality is twisted and recast in the process.

During the writing process, that question, "What myth are you telling?" helps me pin down earlier what the main plot of action is in the story, what themes or moral questions I might be investigating, or where I might locate the most pressing emotions and desires that move my characters to action. Framing one's modern existence within mythical frameworks is not only a way of understanding the world and your potential place in it, but is a way of becoming a part of a larger cycle or story. For writers, especially those who might write from an autobiographical stance, being able to recast individual experience to models of collective experience can be one strategy for avoiding self-indulgence and narcissism.

▪▪▪ THE EXERCISE ▪▪▪▪▪▪▪▪▪▪▪▪▪▪▪▪▪▪▪▪▪▪▪▪▪▪▪▪▪▪▪▪

Interview a family member, eliciting as many stories as possible for as long as possible. (If you want to use a story that you already know for this exercise, that's fine, but you're missing out on half the fun. Ponder whether or not you want to bring a notebook, tape recorder, or video camera; each has its own merits, as does simply listening.) Welcome stories that do not involve you directly, as well as those that do.

1. Take one of these stories and try to figure out what myth, fairy tale, or fable it most closely resembles. Think about plot, themes, archetypal characters, morals, and symbols; find correspondences between the family story and your chosen myth, fairy tale, or fable.

2. Write your family story within the conventions of your chosen myth, fable, or fairy tale. Keep in mind that most myths are written in the third person omniscient point of view. This will help you look at the story in a more objective fashion, and will also help you concentrate on plot and action, rather than reflection. Remember also that because you are basing your family story on an earlier, likely better-known story, you can have a lot of fun playing with the two stories, in terms of both similarities and differences, because some of the fun of the story will come from the fact that readers will recognize it as a story that they

already know. (What if Eve had offered Adam a slice of pizza instead of an apple? What if Cinderella played basketball and her prince went out searching for his true love with one lonely sneaker?)If you pick a holiday or family weekend visit, you can conduct this exercise several times with several different family members. You can even get each to tell you the same stories. Pay attention to how the story might be framed differently, or how the details might change, depending on who is telling the story.

SUGGESTED READING

James Joyce's *A Portrait of the Artist as a Young Man* is a wonderful example of how an autobiographical family tale can be recast within a mythological structure. The father–son myth of Icarus and Daedalus runs through the entire story of a boy determined to make his own way in the world and rise through his artistic genius to heights his father could only have imagined. Angela Carter's *The Bloody Chamber* also makes excellent reading as she rewrites fairy tales through the eyes of a modern feminist to fascinating results.

Advice

Families are a wealth of information, and a writer should always value this resource. Take time to ask the various members of your family about their lives, how they feel or felt about their own parents or grandparents, what details they remember about growing up, what they hope to accomplish by a certain age, how the world has changed over their lifetimes thus far, what their greatest pleasures have been, what moments they'd like to return to for a second chance. You will gather together more important things than just stories; you will gather together memories, voices, glimpses of those who are no longer with us but who wish to be acknowledged. One day, your family members won't be around to be asked. One day, neither will you. What each person contains is precious.

YESTERDAY'S NEWS
Priscila Uppal

Like a predictable professor, I'm sending you to the library. Make sure you've scheduled at least an entire afternoon or evening for this adventure. Bring a notebook. Maybe even bring some money for printing and photocopying.

Did I say "adventure" and "library" in the same paragraph? I suppose I did. No, it's not a mistake. Just ignore all those students with their heads in their hands, foreheads clapped to binders, cursing their professors. Unless you want to write about them, of course. I suppose you could. However, I want you to keep going, past all the stacks of books that in and of themselves could surely trigger some interesting stories (*The Big Book of Human Abnormalities, Monastery Sign-Language, Greatest Olympic Tales*), past the large wooden drawers filled with maps of Antarctica and the Mediterranean, past the sound and video library where someone might be watching a Hitchcock flick or listening to calypso, up the stairs to where the periodicals and newspapers are bound or have been copied to microfiche.

This is where I want you to spend the afternoon, flipping pages, turning knobs, from local rags to national dailies and international weeklies. Pick a date that means something to you, either personally or historically. Dates are like talismans; all manner of memories and experiences are dredged up by their evocation. You might pick September 1, 1939 (the famous Auden poem echo), for the start of WWII in Europe. What was covered in Toronto, in New York, in London, in Wisconsin? What were the headlines? What were the facts as known on that day? What were the fears, the anxieties, of government officials, of the regular population, as expressed in articles, editorials, letters? What about a week later in the same print sources?

Or you might pick your birthday. Mine is October 30, 1974. What was the headline on the front page? The weather forecast? What about the horoscope? What were the biggest concerns in your place of birth at the time? What crimes were committed? What stocks were selling? What letters to the editor appear? Notice, too, the changes in how the papers were put together. How many sections? What kind? What was the language like? What were the views on such topics as marriage, free speech, fashion, education, transportation, foreign affairs? Flip to the classifieds. What were people selling? How much did it cost to rent a one-bedroom apartment in your city? Flip again. Births and deaths. Who got married? Who lost a wife? Who baptized another child?

Yesterday's news is your treasure chest for all kinds of information. All manner of human celebration and human misery are contained within these print sources, in both words and photographs. Every headline, every article, and every photograph can unravel in a writer's imagination into a compelling story. The older an article is, the more your imagination needs to work to put everything into context, the more you need to do to exercise that muscle to form a fuller picture. Even if you don't always find the right article for a short story or a novel idea, you will always be *thinking* like a writer as you move back through time.

▪▪▪ THE EXERCISE ▪▪▪▪▪▪▪▪▪▪▪▪▪▪▪▪▪▪▪▪▪▪▪▪▪▪▪▪▪▪▪▪▪▪

Pick a date and look up at least three different print sources published on the same day. Peruse them, noting down any headline, article, or photograph that catches your eye.

1. Try to write a page or two of prose that would reflect the time period and locale(s) that you've picked from your newspapers (i.e., 1940s London or 1965 Saskatchewan). Think about creating authentic physical details, but also authentic emotional ones. What seemed to be on people's minds at the time? What factors could contribute to a sense of stability or instability, for instance? What previous event might still be on the public's mind? What forthcoming event might they be waiting for?

2. Pick a particular newspaper story and create a scene out of its details. What information has been included in the article? How can these facts add up to a "story"? What has been left out of the article? Who might be an additional character in this story? What forces might have converged to create this story? Is this a story that could still happen today? Why or why not, and how might be alluded to in your scene. (Frequently, this is how historical fiction achieves relevancy to our present times. What does the past say about our present?)

3. Pick a headline or photograph and remove it from its historical context: Write a prose piece triggered by the implications of the headline or details of the photograph, but set the piece in contemporary times. Essentially, use the newspaper as a resource to brainstorm ideas, rather than as a source of material.

SUGGESTED READING

Most historical fiction relies on the information provided in newspapers to some extent, no matter what the subject, and many stories that do not at first appear historical, or, in fact, might be quite contemporary, draw facts, source information, and/or inspiration from the newspaper. Political scandals, unsolved crimes, bizarre geographical occurrences, medical breakthroughs—all these can provide a writer with enough material for a short story or a novel, or, at the very least, an authentic detail or description to add to a prose piece concerned with someone or something else altogether. A quick perusal of any bookstore display or bookshelf will likely attest to the value of archival research, particularly newspaper research, in putting together a story. The first three books I spot on a shelf beside my bed that might very well have made use of the newspaper are Andrey Kurkov's *Death and the Penguin,* D.M. Thomas's *The White Hotel,* and Janice Kulyk Keefer's *Thieves.*

Advice

The other place to make sure to visit in the library is the archives and special collections. Archives, both personal and institutional, are inexhaustible resources for writers. Visit several, and get to know the staff. They will help you with your research and, eventually, will tell you when things arrive, or are found, that might interest you.

For inspiration and comfort, ask to see the archives of your favorite writers. Read their letters and diaries; look at the many drafts of your favorite short stories and novels or other writings. When you see how much ink (and doubt and anxiety) went into those pages you now know and love so well, you will feel much better about your own writing and revision process. It can be like having a conversation with a friend who knows what you're going through.

WRITE WHAT YOU DON'T KNOW—AT LEAST, NOT FOR SURE

Toby Litt

In 1970, an American artist called Joe Brainard published a short book called *I Remember,* in which each paragraph began with those two simple words. For example: "I remember the only time I ever saw my mother cry. I was eating apricot pie." *I Remember* was a publishing success, and Joe Brainard followed it with *More I Remember, More I Remember More,* and, perhaps inevitably, *I Remember Christmas.*

I first came across the *I remember* form in a book about the French literary group known as Oulipo (Ouvroir de Littérature Potentielle, or Workshop for Potential Literature). One of the central Oulipo writers was Georges Perec, author of *Life: A User's Manual.* He heard about Brainard's new literary form from Harry Mathews, the only American member of the group. In 1978, Perec published a book about his childhood using the *I remember* form. He called it, as you would expect, *Je me souviens.*

I have real problems with travel writing. Basically, I think it depends on falsely exoticizing wherever is being visited. Everywhere is local to where it is. Customs are never quaint. And so, when, in 2003, I was offered the chance to travel around China by train for a month, I wanted to find some way of doing travel writing and, at the same time, of undoing it. What I came up with, remembering Perec, was this—

■■■ THE EXERCISE ■■■■■■■■■■■■■■■■■■■■■■■■■■■■■■■■■

Pick a place you have never visited before. This does not have to involve international air travel, as China did for me. It could be a public building you have often walked past but never been inside. It could be a store whose goods you've never felt the need to examine. More interestingly, but more problematically, it could be the apartment of someone you know well but have never visited at home. (Obviously, choose someone who would be happy to have you visit them. If you are in a writing group, perhaps you could pair up—this would be on the understanding that neither person had to show the other what they ended up writing. You'll soon see why.)

Taking Joe Brainard's *I remember* form as the anticipated basis for this exercise, you are to begin by writing a balancing section. Each sentence of this section will begin with the words *I expect...* You should write *I expect* as fast as you can, keeping the grammar simple and doing your best to avoid all self-censorship—i.e., it's fine to write, "I expect his/her apartment to smell strongly of rotting fish." Give yourself at least an hour to do this. Aim to write around fifty different sentences beginning with *I expect.*

Then set the exercise aside for at least a couple of weeks. Don't open the file or look at the pages again. Instead, try as much as possible to forget what you have written.

To continue the exercise, go and visit the previously unvisited place. Take your time. Sniff around. See whatever there is to see. What you are *not* trying to do is tick off an *I expect* checklist.

Now, leave it for a couple more weeks before you start writing your *I remember*. (And, of course, resist the temptation immediately to look back at your *I expect*.) Give yourself the same amount of uninterrupted time to write *I remember* as you took for *I expect*. Write fast. Do the exact same number of sentences. Don't self-censor.

If you want, you can now read the two sections alongside one another. But if you really have strong willpower, I would leave them both unlooked-at for another couple of weeks.

Also, there is a famous essay by Henry James called "The Art of Fiction". It is reprinted in *The Critical Muse: Selected Literary Criticism* (Penguin). In the essay, James says, "Therefore, if I should certainly say to a novice, 'Write from experience and experience only,' I should feel that this was rather a tantalizing monition if I were not immediately to add, 'Try to be one of the people on whom nothing is lost!'" That's the crux. But the rest of the essay is a wonderful alternative to the simplistic limitations of *write what you know*. This exercise should help you to look much more closely at what you do know, and what you don't.

SUGGESTED READING

Joe Brainard, *I Remember*, Granary Books.

The Oulipo Compendium, edited by Harry Matthews and Alastair Brotchie.

Advice

The good thing about this exercise is that you can use it as a way of making even the most boring place fascinating. If you are forced to go and stay with dull friends or relatives, do an *I expect* in advance. Make it grotesquely detailed. Include smells.

FIVE RULES FOR WRITERS

Kate Pullinger

I think we need more rules. Rules for writers. If I were King of the World, there would be no novels over four hundred pages. Five hundred pages max. Okay, one of the most enjoyable books I've read in the last decade was pushing a thousand pages, but … anyway. Here are my rules:

1. **Never use adjectives and adverbs.** Oh lord, don't get me started. Adjectives and adverbs are for lazy writers. Well, maybe not adjectives, but adverbs definitely, I said brightly. I gazed longingly at her adverb-free piece of writing.

2. **Never use exposition.** Don't explain things to us; we readers don't like to have things explained to us. We like to see things, we like to imagine things, we like to draw our own conclusions, we like to be illuminated, we like enigma and mystery. We don't like to be told what to think.

3. **Never use the words *seem* (and its evil cousins *seemed* and *seems*) and *just*.** Beginner writers just always seem to rely very heavily on these two words. *Just* is like a verbal tic, I think; we hear it in our heads, so we put it on the page.

Just stop. *Seemed,* well, either something is like something else, or it isn't. Be definite. Be specific. Vagueness is your enemy (NB: Vagueness is not the same thing as enigma and mystery).

4. **Never repeat words ... unless you are going for a specific, repetitive style or voice.** I once worked on a novel with a terrific editor who could tell me precisely how many times I had used the word *green,* and on what pages. Nothing drives me crazier than writers who think that because novels have tons of words in them, they can be lazy about word choices, patterns, and rhythms. Every word counts in a novel, like in a short story, like in a poem.

5. **Never ignore the little voice in your head that says, "Oh, that doesn't quite work."** A big part of learning to write (and for me this is an ongoing process) is figuring out the difference between the loud internal voice that says, "THIS IS ALL RUBBISH AND YOU SHOULD NEVER WRITE ANOTHER WORD EVER AGAIN" and that somewhat quieter internal voice that says, "Hmm, that's not quite right, but let's pretend we didn't notice." Learn to trust your gut instinct—listen to that little voice, while ignoring the big, pushy one.

Writing is a kind of confidence trick—you have to convince yourself you can do it, while at the same time telling yourself you can do it better. But you can do it better, and when you do it well, it is very exciting.

Some writers whose work I admire, and who adhere to these rules include Barbara Gowdy, Lynne Tillman, Philip Roth (except for his female characters—oh boy), and Don Delillo (except for that great huge novel that everyone apart from me loved).

FIVE TIPS

Lee Gowan

1. **Ritualize your writing.** Make the time, the place, the atmosphere all part of your personal religion. If writing three mornings a week at nine o'clock works for you, then make sure you write those three mornings every week. I currently have a day job and a seven-year-old, so what works for me is getting up at six, making a pot of tea, and sitting down at the computer. Before I started doing this, I was beginning to feel resentful towards my day job and other commitments, but now I've written a page of my novel before I've had my breakfast, and that makes the rest of the day feel much easier. My resentments have melted away and I'm a better person. Well, not really. But it is better. Even if I am nodding off by ten. In the morning.

    I always listen to music, often turned up fairly loud. When I was writing my last novel I listened to all three volumes of The Magnetic Fields' *69 Love Songs* almost every day. It was my ritual, and just hearing that album still makes me feel like writing. I used to play five games of computer solitaire every day before I started writing. That worked for me, but somewhere along the way I gave it up. Just as well: sometimes when I lost, I'd make the five games turn into ten. And so on.

It doesn't really matter what the rituals are, just so long as they get you in the mood that feels like you should write something down.

2. **Read.** Nothing will teach you more about writing than reading. Read as widely and as deeply as you possibly can, and think like the writer you are while you read. Ask yourself, how did she make me believe that? How come he failed to make me believe? But don't borrow your characters from other people's writing. There have got to be enough characters in your own life.

3. **Listen to Your characters.** You've created them. You are their God and they're praying to You, if only You'll listen. Hear their voices, their dreams, their fears and obsessions. Give them Your love, even Your villains. But resist the temptation to get involved in their affairs, even if they beg You to deliver them from evil. You're a god that has given free will to Your creations. If You're tempted to let the story dictate their actions, making them into puppets, stop Yourself and listen. They're talking to You.

4. **Recognize the power of places and things.** It doesn't matter whether it's a landscape or a kitchen, the setting of your work should always be carefully considered for its resonances and carefully polished with those resonances in mind. Look around the room. Every object is a symbol. No cigar is ever just a cigar. On the other hand, if you allow it into your story or poem, it had better be a real cigar first and foremost, and the baby smoking it had better know her cigars.

5. **Never take advice from other writers.** Writing is different for everyone and they can't possibly know what it's like for you.

HOW TO WRITER-PROOF YOUR LIFE

Elizabeth Ruth

When you decide to fit your life around your writing rather than fit your writing into the cracks of your life, people are bound to react. Lovers may feel displaced. Friends who are frustrated by their own unrealized ambitions may intimate that you are nervy, spoilt, to follow your own writing path. Children, if you have them, will need to learn to respect the chunks of time you now require for your fiction. Family members may not understand what it is you do for all those hours at the computer, but they will worry about how you'll pay the rent (or whether you'll be hitting them up for it). You may even chide yourself for having the ego strength to call yourself a writer. There's no way around it: writing fiction is a risky endeavor on many levels, with no guarantees of material success. However, if you measure success in terms of that risk, and the leap of faith it takes to fill one blank page after another with a whole other universe, you will indeed be rich. So, you must do everything you can to protect your identity as a writer and to protect your writing time.

When new parents are expecting, they inevitably receive unsolicited advice from other parents. Eventually someone suggests childproofing the home—softening sharp corners on tables, covering electrical outlets to avoid disaster, blocking off access to stairwells, and generally creating a welcome living environment that is conducive to a fragile new being. Everything will seem to revolve around Baby. Stories and novels are in need of a similar kind of myopic attention if they are to grow and develop, and beginning-stage writers need to learn how to writer-proof their lives to make this possible. We've all heard Virginia Woolf's famous cry for a "room of one's own," but a writer needs more than privacy (and money). You must take your work seriously or no one else will. You must answer the comments and complaints brought forward by disgruntled loved ones who now find less of your time devoted to meeting their needs. You must realize that, unlike most other tasks in life, writing cannot be delegated. If you don't write your story, it will simply never be born.

▪▪▪ THE EXERCISE ▪▪▪▪▪▪▪▪▪▪▪▪▪▪▪▪▪▪▪▪▪▪▪▪▪▪▪▪▪▪▪▪▪

The following is a list of ten things to help you writer-proof your life. I have done all of these and others, yet it remains a challenge to hold back the wider world from intruding on my time. You will need harsh discipline, fierce determination, and a resolute lack of guilt.

1. If you are writing full time, treat it like the job that it is. Show up at your desk at 9:00 a.m., dressed (pajamas will do) and ready to begin. Work from nine to five, with a short lunch break. If you are not able to write full time, rise two hours early, before everyone else. Set a daily word limit for yourself;

for example, a thousand words. Writers don't wait for inspiration. If we did, we'd be waiting a mighty long time.

Writing is hard work. It's a job. Treat it as such.

2. If you have a habit of keeping a diary or writing in a journal, break it. Many writers keep "morning pages" and try to jump-start their creativity in this way. It usually doesn't work, and it definitely eats into precious fiction-writing hours. If you are wedded to the idea of journaling, I suggest you relegate it to the end of the day, and keep your fresh brain for the hard task of fiction. You're going to need all the help you can get!

3. I like to use music to ease me into a mood. For example, my novel *Smoke* was set in the 1950s, and I listened to the *Platters*'s version of "Smoke Gets in Your Eyes" over and over. There was an aching simplicity and quality of longing in that song that I wanted to capture in my writing. Music can have a trancelike effect that is highly conducive to accessing fiction.

4. The internet may be a useful research and fact-checking tool for people who don't like libraries, but email is the bane of any writer's existence. Email can suck up the better part of a day. It's the enemy of fiction writing. Hearing and feeling the click-clack of the keyboard under your fingers as you type emails can make you feel like a writer without you actually being one. If you write using a computer that is used for email, be sure to turn off the sound that announces new messages. My rule: never check email before 5:00 p.m.

5. Get rid of your television, or at least do yourself a favor and don't get cable. With only two or three local channels to watch, you are unlikely to find yourself distracted from your

writing by reality TV and bad sitcoms. I have twice packed up the TV and put it in storage for long stretches. Television kills imagination.

6. Unplug the phone before you begin writing. I have the same reaction to the telephone as I do to the doorbell: if someone is calling, they are clearly alive and therefore there is no real emergency.

7. If you live with other people, sit them down and explain that from now on you will be taking your writing more seriously. Explain that you will therefore have less free time for socializing, but that you will be happier when you do because you will have been productive. Explain that when the door to your writing room is closed, no one is to enter. (If someone tests this rule, all you need to do is rant and rave and generally behave like a mad person and it won't happen again—trust me.)

8. If you are responsible for feeding other members of the household, learn to cook in bulk and freeze meals. I like to cook on Sundays, large pots of stew-like things. Thaw something several times a week and presto! You've saved three or four hours for your writing.

9. Lower your standards. Unlike a brilliant, fleeting idea, a sink full of dishes and a pile of dirty laundry can wait. Ignoring mundane household chores for as long as possible never hurt anyone, but not finishing your writing project will hurt you.

10. Post all rejection letters (and you'll receive a few) on the wall. Treat them like wallpaper. That's about how meaningful they are. After a while you won't even notice them. Similarly, post all good reviews and look at them frequently. Big yourself up. No one else will.

SUGGESTED READING

You have only to look at the career of any prolific fiction writer to know they mastered the art of writer-proofing their lives. John Irving, Margaret Atwood, Joyce Carol Oates, Dionne Brand, Timothy Findley, Jeanette Winterson. If you read their work, you'll find breadth, depth, texture, and originality, and you'll know that their books could not have come from the margins of the writer's life—they had to have been at its center.

Advice

No one cares—or will care—as much about your writing as you do (not agents, not editors, not lovers, not your mother), so be prepared to spend hours crafting it, and uncomfortable moments defending and promoting it. Your stories may be the one thing you do on this lonely planet that belongs irrevocably to you. Don't rush, don't be afraid of time.

EDITING WITH COLOR
Elizabeth Ruth

Any professional writer will tell you that revision and editing consume the majority of our time. We write and rewrite whole drafts, nipping and tucking, rethinking, adjusting plot, killing off characters, collapsing two characters into one, removing adjectives one week and adding choice adjectives the next. Arguably, it's a neurotic's job, but someone's got to do it. We give shape to the story in the early drafts (and they're often quite drafty!) getting it all down on the page, forming a skeleton of sorts, and then we face the hard task of adding flesh to those bones, enhancing sense of place, making sure dialogue is crisp and authentic, and that character development follows a logical and reasonable path, ensuring there is sufficient dramatic tension and that our central themes and metaphors are effective and fresh. Much of this happens through revision.

Each writer—you included—has a particular editorial process, though it is rarely articulated. Some writers run each sentence or paragraph through their mind many times before committing it to paper, or they edit as they write, paragraph by paragraph, painstakingly getting it right as they go. Others devote the first phase of the writing process to simply getting the story out in an unbroken flow, with no serious attention paid to either substantive editing or copyediting. It doesn't matter how you edit—though there is no way around the fact that all stories need revision. It is not uncommon for me to put a completed draft away in my desk drawer for a period of time—two weeks, say, or a year—and return to it with fresh eyes, precisely for the purpose of an effective edit. The author sits too close to the material to identify every editorial need. Sometimes I have a trusted writer friend review my completed draft, hoping he or she will catch things I've missed. You may have a professional editor waiting in the wings, but if you are wise, you will not hand off a manuscript unless it has been worked and reworked to the best of your ability. The professional editor, who is certainly invaluable, comes in at a late stage, but it is always your responsibility, as the writer, to bring the body of work to maturity.

Editing is not a flashy, glamorous subject, though the rewards for well-polished words are immeasurable. Your writing will be clean and clear and therefore more likely to receive an offer of publication. Once it does, you can stand solidly behind it, knowing you gave it your full time and attention, confident that you can move on to the next story that beckons.

▪▪▪ THE EXERCISE ▪▪▪▪▪▪▪▪▪▪▪▪▪▪▪▪▪▪▪▪▪▪▪▪▪▪▪▪▪▪▪▪▪▪

In addition to the standard slash-and-burn marking up of pages that we all use to edit our writing, I have developed an unusual technique to edit for point of view and for plot that works well in the final stages of a project. This exercise originated after a visual artist friend of mine suggested that I would notice new things in the fiction if I found a way to view my work with a less linear editorial eye, to "see" my stories from the outside—rather than simply from deep within. For lack of a better name, the technique I've developed can be referred to as *editing with color*. Here's how it works:

1. Buy a package of multicolored thick magic markers.

2. Clear as much floor space as you can in your office. If you don't have an office, use the kitchen floor or basement floor, and arrange to be alone in the house or apartment.

3. Print off each page of your manuscript. Set each page down, in the order it's meant to be read, beginning in the top left-hand corner of the room and proceeding across the floor and then down a row and across again. Your room effectively becomes a giant page. The goal here is to see the entire project *at once*, rather than page by page as you do when you edit the traditional way. (I live in a small space and primarily write novels, so I assure you that it is possible to set down four hundred pages.) If you run out of floor space, do the first half of the manuscript and then repeat the exercise for the second half. I have also done this when I've only had enough space for one chapter at a time.

4. *Editing with color* works well for a story written in the third person, because in the third person you're moving in and out of different characters' points of view and need to make sure to linger for an adequate length of time on each. The reader needs to feel a connection to a given character before you slip away to be with someone else. To verify that you have a balanced presentation of point of view, assign each central figure in your manuscript a color. For example, Joe = red, Jill = blue, Betty = green.

5. Read through your manuscript on the floor, and highlight all passages pertaining to Joe, Jill, and Betty in the assigned colors. It sounds too obvious to be of much use, but the impact of

standing back once you've highlighted the entire piece and reading *visually* can be profound. You will immediately notice abrupt shifts in point of view, and a disproportionate time spent on one character versus another. You will be editing with a different eye, and that is always a good thing.

■ ■ ■ ■ ■ ■ ■

The second way that I have found *editing with color* useful is when looking at plot. If you have set your novel in two places— for example, Paris and New York—and you want to make sure you have given adequate attention to each setting, color the Paris passages in purple and the New York passages in yellow. You will immediately note that, despite the important event that takes place for your protagonist in Paris, you have hurried your travels there and only given half as much space to that city as compared with the New York scenes. By noting, in color, when you switch from one locale to another, you will also be able to evaluate whether you've made too many switches, and you'll make a more conscious choice about the structure of telling. For example, you may see that intuitively you have had the novel alternate chapters between Paris and New York, with the exception of a few instances, and you may decide to clean the structure up so that it is a true and consistent alternating of chapters.

Editing with color sounds more mechanical and cumbersome than it is. Perhaps it even strikes you as too self-conscious; however, I encourage you to try it—or develop your own spin-off. I have used this editorial process with both of my novels, and a few short stories, and I have taught my students to use this technique. It's a fun reprieve from the linearity of a traditional edit, and you are guaranteed to notice something that you otherwise would have missed.

SUGGESTED READING

Since *editing with color* is something I've developed for myself, I can only point to my own work as published examples. In *Ten Good Seconds of Silence,* I used color to structure the order of telling. The novel dealt with memory and time and so flashed backward and forward, alternating chapters between two cities and two time periods. My second novel, *Smoke,* was a more straightforward telling, but I used color to identify and control switches in an intimate third person narrative.

Advice

Writing is really just the elusive art of capturing your soul for a brief instant and translating it onto a page. It's impossible, but if you're committed, you will go on trying. Probably, despite the advice of other writers, you will find your own idiosyncratic way forward.

INTERVIEW
Steve Almond

What do you expect the first few paragraphs of a short story to accomplish?

There's a million different ways a story can be told, so I don't want to sound prescriptive. But I will say that almost all readers come to stories (whether four pages or four hundred) with two basic questions:

1. Who do I care about?
2. What do they care about?

This intensity of feeling (whether desire, fear, or some combination of the two) is what keeps us reading a story. So I try to answer these two questions as soon as I can. I'm also grateful when writers establish the concrete aspects of the story: where we are, what we're going to hear about.

Young writers have a tendency to hold back basic info from the reader, usually because they lack the faith required to tell the story straight. They feel that keeping secrets from the reader—for instance, that the main character has inoperable cancer—will guarantee interest. I cannot begin to express how wrong this notion is.

The Hippocratic oath of writing is: Never confuse the reader. Don't make him or her waste energy trying to understand what's happening.

There's also a huge difference between surprise and suspense. Let's say I started a story with this line:

On the day Dave Roderick was brutally murdered, his wife gave birth to a beautiful baby girl.

I have just given away the two major plot elements of the story. That doesn't mean the reader loses interest. The mystery resides in how and why things happen.

Describe a typical writing day—what's your process?

I try to write in the mornings, because I'm freshest then—or at least fresh from my dream world, which is where the subconscious has the chance to rule the roost. My hope is always to get a few hours of work done early, because otherwise I feel guilty for the rest of the day. This usually doesn't happen, so I spend the next ten to twelve hours feeling guilty and bouncing around my apartment in a state of restless anxiety. Really, it's a great way to make a living!

I try to read every day, and to avoid TV at all costs—it's such a powerful energy sucker. When possible, I exercise. (Pacing does not count as exercise.) I eat a good deal of chocolate.

But the truth is, everyone has his or her own process. When people ask me about this, I usually say: whatever keeps your ass in the chair, that's your process.

You've written in a number of different forms—short story, novel, nonfiction, epistolary novel, linked stories—can you tell about your experience of each?

I'm primarily a short story writer. That feels like the most natural way that we tell stories, whether around the campfire or in the bar or wherever; we say, "This crazy thing happened to me..." There's also an intensity to short stories, an emotional urgency that I've not been able to sustain in my many failed novels.

In fact, all of my writing boils down to this: telling the truth about something that matters to me deeply. It doesn't matter especially if it's fiction or nonfiction, a poem or an epistolary novel. What matters is the extent to which I sympathize with (love, actually) the people I'm writing about. And my willingness to expose them to emotional danger, and stick with them in their time of need.

Is it harder to sell a collection of stories to a publisher?

It's much harder to sell a collection of stories, for the simple reason that there's a much smaller paying audience. Any serious story writer, such as George Saunders or Charles D'Ambrosio, gets asked constantly: Where's the novel? Everyone in publishing wants the novel. Because novels are considered bigger and more ambitious, and because (on the whole) they sell better. I've dealt with this pressure throughout my career.

So, people regard the short story as an "apprentice" form, something you do to prep yourself for the novel. The irony is that the prose in published story collections tends to be stronger than in novels, because the barrier to publication is so much higher.

My own pet theory is that short stories aren't more popular because they make too much of an emotional demand on the reader: they pack the emotion and consequence into a much smaller number of words.

Then again, this could be my rationalization, as someone who keeps writing wretched novels and stuffing them in drawers.

What steps do you advise a new writer to take on the path toward publication?

The single most important task for any young writer is to learn how to critique your own work. You have to develop what Hemingway called a "bullshit detector," which allows you to see where you're pushing the language too hard, confusing the reader, rushing through moments that should be sustained. The way this happens generally is that you see the mistakes other young writers make. As a rule, you're too close to your own work to see the problems.

The best thing I ever did, learning-wise, was to edit a literary magazine in grad school. I read more than a thousand stories in a single year, most of them by other beginning writers. After a while, I could see all the mistakes—the overwriting, the clichés, the emotional evasions—and I started recognizing them in my own work. That's why, when I teach, I place the central emphasis on the task of critiquing other student work. That's how you develop a critical faculty.

I'd also suggest that young writers think **as little as possible** about getting an agent or connecting with editors or the rest of that networking stuff. Learn how to critique your own work. The rest will follow.

What is your experience of writing a female character versus a male character?

To be honest, the gender (or race or class) of my characters isn't essential. It's just the particular furniture of a story. What matters is the internal life of my people: what they're up against, what they fear, what they desire. If I can identify those things, I'm good to go.

That being said, I do enjoy writing from a female point of view, because I think most women (to make a huge, ridiculous, but also accurate generalization) live closer to their emotions than men. They naturally ask the sort of questions that good stories ask: How and why did things go wrong? What hurt most? Why do I feel like I do?

If you ever get stumped in your writing, what are your methods for getting writing again?

No easy answer here. Writers get blocked for a couple of reasons. First, because they lose interest in their material, lose the sense of curiosity and compassion that binds them to the fate of their characters. And second, because the self-punitive part of their psyches overwhelms the self-loving part.

So, one thing I try to do when I'm struggling is to lower the pressure. I just tell myself: this isn't going to be a good writing day; that doesn't make you a failure, put the gun back in the drawer. I also try to remind myself that what I'm working on is a draft. It's not the finished work that the world will see. When people get blocked, it's really a form of freezing up. You become self-conscious on the page and start editing the truth. You have to find that emotional state where you can forgive yourself whatever mistakes you're going to make and relax and let it rip.

What's your feeling about teaching creative writing?

I love it. And I learn an incredible amount from my students. Mostly, I'm just inspired that people who are twenty-one or twenty-two years old have the courage to write creatively. It took me until I was nearly thirty years old to work up that kind of nerve. And there are always one or two students every term who blow me away.

There are some folks who try to badmouth teaching creative writing, as if the pursuit were dependent on some divine received wisdom, or simply a matter of individual struggle. But most young writers need a sense of shared mission, some guidance, the reassurance—in the face of a semi-literate culture that worships fame and convenience—that the lonely, dogged work of writing is vital. That's what MFA programs provide: they are welfare states for young artists. They help writers (like me) take their creative work more seriously. The real work is still up to the person at the keyboard.

How important is it for a new writer to have an agent?

That's tough for me to answer, because for most of my career I've not had an agent. And, as I noted, a lot of young writers come to believe that getting an agent will mean they've "made it." They invest far too much time and energy in worrying about this, and invest their agents with far too much power.

Agents can be extremely helpful. They can serve as a gateway, and help young writers negotiate the various mazes of publishing. They can look after the business aspects of a writer's career, so the writer can focus on his or her art. All laudable.

But agents are just brokers: they present art to the commercial powers. They might grant writers a certain kind of access, but important work will find a way into the world, because that's what editors are looking for. They don't care who delivers the package; they want the goods.

What is the biggest challenge for you to do with your writing?

First on my list is to write a novel on my own. I've been unable to make it happen yet, but I'm still slugging away. That's all you can do: slug away.

The broader challenge, one that faces all writers, is to reassert the majesty and relevance of reading in this culture. That sounds grandiose, but it's the truth. This species is goose-stepping toward self-destruction, in part because we've lost touch with our moral imaginations.

Look, there's no shortage of writers in this world. What we lack is the capacity to attend and to feel, the deep concentration that reading demands.

And this challenge is mine, as an individual: to ignore the childish distractions, the flashing BUY signs, that pass for a civic culture today. And to continue to devote myself to the greater compassion that art creates and demands.

EVERY PICTURE TELLS A STORY...?

Steven Hayward

There is a photograph of the author that shows him at age seventeen with a blue guitar. He is not looking directly into the camera because this is 1987, a year when guitar players everywhere decide, on the basis of the recently released *The Joshua Tree* (in which not one of the band members stares back at the camera), it is best to avert one's gaze. The sun is intensely bright, and he squints into the distance, half-smiling despite his efforts not to, his white, uneven teeth poking out and looking whiter for the sunlight. Because of his squint, you cannot see that his left eye is crossed; the following summer, surgery will correct the defect, and then, not quite two weeks after that, he will lose his virginity.

The patch will still be on his eye, but it will seem to him as if the operation has worked its magic already, done exactly what the smiling surgeon at the big Toronto hospital promised it would. Next to him are the other band members, all of them in leather jackets and stone-washed blue jeans, all wearing tremendously large belt buckles. The author is holding his blue guitar up, as if for our inspection, left hand at the neck, bending a string. One could say the author is arrested at a moment of happiness, although photographs, because they exclude everything except the second in which they are snapped, always lie. Still one stares, wanting it to give up its truth; one wishes to see, trapped forever in the author's eyes, the image of the photographer, to know whether the irregular shadow on the fallen leaves surrounding the line of boys is his father, the owner of the front lawn on which they are standing, or the author's old friend, Chris, who played saxophone, but never well enough to be in the band and became instead their manager until twelfth grade when, early one Sunday morning, he froze, drunk, in the late January snow.

■■■ THE EXERCISE ■■■■■■■■■■■■■■■■■■■■■■■■■■■■■■■■■■■

Find a photo of yourself that is interesting enough to write about. By "interesting" I mean contradictory—a picture that pulls in more than one direction at the same time.

Write a 450-word paragraph describing it, making sure to

1. Write it in the present tense, because everything in a photo is always happening now; you may get old, die, but you will still be young and beautiful and dancing with Kathy in that photo (show us, in other words, the horrible selectivity of photos, the way they are a slice of the now, but only the now).

2. Include in the paragraph, somewhere, an interrupted gesture (the ball about to be caught, the string in the middle of the bend, the moment just before the hands touch).

3. Make some reference to the future of the photograph, to what the frame cuts out in a temporal way (among other

things, this will require you to use the future perfect tense, to say things like "The author will, some fifteen years later, still have extremely tiny feet").

4. Bring up the person who is taking the photo.

5. Refer to the death of at least one person in the photo (this, of course, is entirely optional, but studies have shown that one's writing gets 46 percent better as soon as it's secretly about someone who's dead or who's about to be dead).

SUGGESTED READING

Look at the middle chapter of Julian Barnes's *A History of the World in 10 ½ Chapters;* he's talking about a painting and it's longer than four hundred words, but you'll get the idea. Or, and this is really what made me want to write about photos in my own work, see Margaret's Atwood's poem, "This is a Photograph of Me."

Advice

The photo really exists: taken in the fall of 1987, the band was called Changeling. I played guitar. But that's all that's true. In writing about the photo, I've changed it. Fictionalized it. Made it tell a story. That's the real task. If, when you're writing, you find there's stuff not in your photo but should be, put it in. No one will know. The author, for example, was never a virgin.

GETTING STARTED

Steven Hayward

There's nothing better than writing when your writing is going well; there's nothing worse when it's not. Is there anything more terrible than sitting around with your arms crossed, waiting to get started on a new project? Sometimes it actually seems impossible. Even when I've had enough sleep and there's nothing on TV, even when I *think* I have something to say—a story to tell—it's no guarantee that good writing will be the result. I'll sit down and everything will seem stale and tired and predictable and worn and written by someone who had no business thinking he could write anything in the first place. You know what I mean. On the other hand, there are times when the opposite happens: when I sit down, *convinced* that nothing good will come of it, and find myself swept up in a story. What's the secret? I don't know, but I wish I did. One thing I am sure of is that all writers know what it feels like to think they will never write anything ever again. It's at such moments, when beginning seems impossible, that exercises like the following come in handy. It might not lead into the great work you know is inside of you, but it will get you writing. And once you are writing, anything can happen.

▪▪▪ THE EXERCISE ▪▪▪▪▪▪▪▪▪▪▪▪▪▪▪▪▪▪▪▪▪▪▪▪▪▪▪▪▪▪▪

1. Begin with a character. Give that character a name.

2. Next, create a second character who has a significant relationship with the first. Give that character a name.

3. Maroon these two characters in a place you've been to more than three times. (I don't mean actually maroon, but I do think the occasion of these two characters intersecting with each other needs to have the flavor of their being stranded, of a break from what usually happens or should happen. Life happens one day at a time; literature takes place on that one day that happens that one time.)

4. Next, give your first character some life-changing news.

5. Write a page or two about what happens between your two characters.

SUGGESTED READING

I first learned about this exercise from my friend Sarah Willis, a novelist who wrote, among others, a very fine novel called *Some Things That Stay*. This novel—her first (she's now written five!)—began as this very writing exercise in a workshop that was being directed by Karen Joy Fowler, who wrote *The Jane Austen Book Club*. Karen passed it to Sarah, who passed it to me—and now I pass it to you. That is the way writers work. Which is not to say they aren't competitive. They are. It's just that the whiteness of the page is that bad. Give your good writing prompts away—what matters is what comes from them.

Advice

If you're still having trouble getting started, try giving your first character the name of someone you know. It's better if it's someone you neither love nor hate. What you want, in the end, is a character whom you can think about with a certain amount of objectivity. You'll need to change those names once the exercise starts, to take you in the direction it's supposed to take you—toward a fully realized work of fiction—but sometimes using the name of a real person can get the machinery working.

GET THE WORDS RIGHT

Antanas Sileika

I read about five hundred samples of student writing every year and 85 percent of the work gives itself away as amateurish within the first page. I'm not complaining—these students have come to find out how to make their work better, and that's what my school does.

The problem is more serious if a writer is submitting to a magazine or book publisher. Most agents and publishers can reject the majority of submissions on the basis of a cover letter or a first page. For a hilarious and painful example, see Will Ferguson's *Happiness™*, in which a cynical and jaded editor tosses out manuscripts because of minor redundancies such as this: "I am sending along my fictional novel…" Anybody in the writing business has seen "fictional novel" submissions. The editor need not read on. This redundancy reveals a writer as amateurish and ignorant. *Reject*.

Every agent or publisher who has ever spoken at my school has said the same thing. He or she reads tentatively, line by line, ready to put aside an awkward text.

Editors' tastes in writing vary widely, some preferring lyrical prose and some preferring lean, minimalist sentences in the manner of Raymond Carver. But no literary editor or agent will ever pick up material that has redundancies, persistent and repeated grammar errors, jargon, or clichés. Every writing book tells us as much, but why is it so hard to write clean prose? Because we speak in redundancies, clichés, and jargon. The prose that is going to make your career must be fresh, and in order for it to be fresh, it must be swept clean.

Take, for example, the following phrase:

"I'm tired," he thought to himself.

This is the kind of thing that I have seen hundreds of times. I submit that it is bad prose, even though it looks like ordinary language.

First, why are thoughts being delivered as dialogue? Unless there is some overriding stylistic reason for this, thoughts are not spoken out loud and so should be put straight into the prose, resulting in this:

He was tired, he thought to himself.

Second, let's scrutinize this a little more for redundancy. We can ask ourselves, who else could he think to? Therefore, we can simplify the sentence further:

He was tired, he thought.

Third, this sentence should sound a little awkward to the ear. You could flip it, but if you did, you might introduce the idea of doubt. Therefore, strip away the ambiguity, and you come up with this sentence:

He was tired.

Finally, I propose that this sentence is better than the first. It is simple and direct. You will need something else in your prose or you will bore an editor, but at least you won't irritate her.

I cannot overstate this: bad writing irritates the reader and prevents her from seeing your genius in plot, character development, atmosphere, etc.

Of course, there is more to line editing than removing errors and redundancies. You must look for consistency of tone, clarity, elimination of generalizations, and many other elements of good prose. At very least, though, your sentences must be clean.

Let's look at an example that was brought in to me by a student who was angry and horrified at the changes her editor had made to her work. The student had written something like this:

My grandmother nurtured me more than any of my other relatives, including my mother.

The word that stuck in the editor's craw, and mine, was "nurture." This is a generalizing term, one you might find in psychology or sociology, or worse, on a greeting card.

Most writers work by intuition, and most professional writers' intuition would immediately eliminate "nurture" because it feels wrong, giving a warm and vague connotation. But the word can be attacked for more concrete reasons. It shows, at best, a generalizing tendency. It is used as an umbrella to cover everything from baking cookies, to hugging, to reading stories aloud, to simply listening attentively. A general term is not vivid. It is dull. At worst, a writer uses words such as this one to save herself the trouble of writing many sentences or even pages that demonstrate the nurturing qualities of the grandmother.

How do you shear this type of language from your prose? Reread it many times, under different circumstances. Read it aloud. Ask yourself, with as much diligence as you can, "Have I found the right word?"

A warning: this is definitely not part of the first draft process. If you watch yourself too carefully as you are composing a first draft, you will inhibit yourself and freeze up, maybe even forming a writers' block. You should save your pruning shears for second and subsequent drafts.

▪▪▪ THE EXERCISE ▪▪▪▪▪▪▪▪▪▪▪▪▪▪▪▪▪▪▪▪▪▪▪▪▪▪▪▪▪▪▪▪▪▪

1. Take a page of your writing and interrogate each word for generalization, cliché, redundancy, generalization, and tone. Make cuts and changes

2. Imagine you have been instructed by your editor to reduce the words on the page by a third. Do it. Compare the two pages the following day and decide which is better, building up from the reduced version again if necessary.

3. See the first page of my story "Going Native" (on page 97) as it was edited by a very good, very tough editor.

    (Incidentally, most unpublished writers are unaware of just how many changes are made by editors. I, and most writers I know, have had entire pages cut, leaving a single sentence. Most writers benefit from this editorial intervention.)

SUGGESTED READING

1. Read the opening page of Oliver Sacks's *Uncle Tungsten: Memories of a Chemical Boyhood* for an example of an exquisite first page that is concrete and vivid and does not waste a word.

2. Read the chapter on revision in Janet Burroway's excellent *Writing Fiction* (sixth edition).

3. Read the two versions of the Raymond Carver story, "So Much Water, So Close To Home," available in *About These Stories* (McGraw Hill). Decide whether the shorter version has been shorn too much.

4. If you are lucky enough to know an editor or a professional writer, ask to see a piece that has been marked up and taken through various drafts.

Advice

This exercise is very important as it will eliminate unintentional gaffes. However, your work still needs to be interesting in some way, compelling and fresh. There is more to writing than eliminating errors, but you must eliminate the errors before the words can sing the tune you have chosen to play.

Going Native

Stan was a DP like my father, like the rest of us, but the out-house had made even him laugh. Not the outhouse itself, although it was the only one in the subdivision growing up in the old orchards, but the neat squares of newspaper my father had us stack beside the seat.

"You such a fucking DP," Stan said to my father, and he held his sides as he laughed like a character out of a cartoon. Stan only swore when he spoke English, a language that didn't really count.

in full.
we are not a
family newspaper

My father went out and bought two rolls of toilet paper, but for half a year we used them only as decoration, like twin flower vases. Stan's advice on toilet paper and anything else in this foreign land was reliable. As for what the locals advised, one could never be sure. Their way of life was strange enough. But within this strangeness were odd people - those who might advise you not from the authority of their culture, but from some kind of disturbed centre.

This sounds
pompous —
clashes with
DP-ness.

"A fool is always dangerous," my father told me, "but a foreign fool is worse. You can't tell if he's an idiot or simply a foreigner."

Mr. Taylor was the only real Canadian we knew in the dawn of our subdivision, and we watched him as if we were anthropologists trying to decipher the local customs.

this word can
only be used
of writing -
just use
understand
or some
such

fathom

Mr. Taylor was a special kind of Canadian, an "English". They were the only kind who really counted, and observation of them could pay a dividend. Mr. Taylor was *our* English, the one who lived across the street and whose habits could be observed at will. We were astonished that he kept on his dress shirt and pants as he read the evening paper in a lawn chair in his back yard. The lawn chair was just as astonishing. Who else but an English would spend good money on a chair that could only be used outside? *My father spent on ground for his...*

can you get
the distinction
clearer?

My father

"These English are just like Germans", my mother sighed. We knew what that was supposed to mean - good - not DP. Only Germans and English of a certain type were not DP. *Not like us, she meant. We belonged on the evolutionary step with the Italians, Poles, and Ukrainians who still knuckles scraped the earth*

"He's a banker," my mother told us, and the word was heavy with meaning. It explained how he lived in a house that not only had proper brick walls and a roof, but a lawn as well. His was the only finished house on our street, and

"You want us to live underground?"
my mother asked, "like moles?
like worms?"
"No," my father said. "Like foxes."

Our street had but a dozen houses... but
between but none of them rest were finished.
a dog a foundations and laid the blocks when a little
money came in. Then they waited and saved for because
joists and studs. The Taylors stood out because a conferma for
built their house. We stood out too an moved in before
who aboveground walls went up

THE FLASHBACK

Greg Hollingshead

A few years ago, the editor of a well-known Canadian literary magazine commented that the most common problem in the stories submitted to the magazine was an overuse, and a misuse, of the flashback. It's significant, I think, that the term itself comes from screenwriters. The primary difficulty of the flashback when it comes to fiction is clear from its definition: an interruption of the continuity of the story by the portrayal or narration of an earlier event. First, the continuity of the story is interrupted. Second, the reader must take a step back in time and start again. Since starting a story in the first place is difficult and stressful enough for most readers, since writers devote most of their energy and skill to keeping the reader engaged with the story, and since readers like to feel they're moving ahead and will naturally resist a narrative step backward, the question is, why are flashbacks so fatally attractive to contemporary fiction writers?

Here are two broad answers to this loaded question. Both are highly debatable.

The first starts with an epigram by Karl Klaus: "Modern literature: prescriptions written by patients." I take this as a comment on the prevalence of Freud's influence—the influence of psychoanalysis—on twentieth-century literature, specifically, here, of the idea that the real story, the crucial story, the one that will reveal the true nature of a character, must be retrieved from the past. We're all damaged in one way or another, and the reason why is to be found in a previous experience, more or less traumatic, probably from childhood. While this insight may be true, or partially true, for many, I suggest it's had an undue influence on modern literature, not just in the limited approach to character it encourages but in this assumption that the authentic narrative, the one that really matters, is not the one we started reading. That in order to understand a character's true motivation, sooner or later we're going to need an embedded past-time narrative.

The other main reason for the prevalence of the flashback is, I believe, the promise of emotional insulation that distant-past-time narration offers to the writer. We're all reluctant to stir up the painful and confusing emotional memories that can be necessary to get a significant dramatic event just right. That's why it's so tempting to put the big break from home, say, or the act or word that crucially failed a friend, in a flashback, to insulate oneself as an artist from the pain of one's own experience in that department, to do it as an event remembered by a character, filtered through a consciousness at a distance of time. The writer's work is so much safer, neater, cleaner, faster, and easier that way. And so much less convincing, engaging, and affecting for the reader. If the flashback you're tempted to use can't be handled briefly, you might want to ask yourself whether that past story, if it's so important, isn't the one you should be telling in the first place, or whether the information available from it can't be communicated within the context of the present story, without reversion to a past-time narrative. And always ask yourself if there isn't something vital, difficult, painful, or plain terrifying about that chunk of story that by casting it as a flashback you're unconsciously trying to avoid.

This said, a well-used flashback is an efficient way to provide motivation for a character. To that end, it should be brief and clear, if not vivid. It should relate emotional, not just material or circumstantial, information. The motivation we're discovering should already have been enacted dramatically in present time, so that the reader is prepared to go there, interested enough to take the step back. Finally, the move in and out of the flashback should be executed as smoothly as possible, neither confusing the reader nor drawing more attention to the device than it will already draw. Like any device that's generally overused or misused, the flashback needs to be handled with care. It needs to be worked on, it needs to be *earned*.

▪▪▪ THE EXERCISE ▪▪▪▪▪▪▪▪▪▪▪▪▪▪▪▪▪▪▪▪▪▪▪▪▪▪▪▪▪▪▪▪▪▪▪▪▪

Harry is arriving late at the office. Somehow that morning, in the brief time between getting up late and rushing from the house, he has managed to have an argument with his wife (or son, or daughter) in which, he knows, he's crossed an unspoken line. There have been fights before this, and the line is a fine one, but in his heart he knows—though he would rather not—that he's crossed it, and that there is nothing he can do that will make that relationship what it was before this morning.

The exercise is to provide a four- to five-hundred word portrait of Harry's emotional state as he arrives at the office at this watershed moment in his life. In the first version, use a 150-word or less flashback, structuring the narrative in such a way that your reader will genuinely want to go there. In the second, write Harry's portrait with no past-time narrative. We will infer how things are with Harry entirely from how he interacts with who and what is around him, and from his thoughts and reflections, without the insertion of a previous-time narrative. Whether by means of a flashback or by the unfolding of Harry's present-time thoughts and interactions, this will be a portrait of a character in the aftermath of crossing a line that has changed his life.

SUGGESTED READING

You can see flashbacks used well in Flannery O'Connor's famous story "Everything That Rises Must Converge." Julian accompanies his mother on the bus to her exercise class at the Y. The story is told from his point of view. As it unfolds, it's clear that his mother's nature, particularly what he views as her racism, angers him. The flashbacks—his memories of a house his grandfather once lived in, of his mother's sacrifices raising and educating him, of his own failed attempts to befriend black people—tell us that Julian is more his mother's son than he understands. While it could be argued that the device of the flashback is not necessary to O'Connor's story, there is no denying that she has used it to clarify and deepen our sense of Julian's motivation, as well as provide a broader social and psychological context for both Julian and his mother. At ten lines or more, O'Connor's flashbacks are somewhat longer than the one I've suggested for the exercise, but her skillful handling of their openings and closings, of their placement, and of the mischievous play of her irony has prevented them feeling like interruptions and kept them poignant and fresh to this day.

Advice

The use of past perfect verbs ("had run") is a simple way to indicate previous time in a simple past tense narrative ("ran"). Use only one or two to open the flashback; once you've established previous time, you don't need to persist with the past perfect; slip back to the simple past form ("ran"). If you want to have conversation in your flashback, consider using indirect rather than direct speech.

METONYMY
Greg Hollingshead

Metonymy is arguably the central device of fiction and one of the most challenging to handle well. A metonym is a kind of metaphor: a related thing that stands for the thing itself. It fulfills two primary requirements of art: indirectness (as opposed to explicitness, to stated meaning) and particularity (as opposed to generalities and abstractions). The connection between the thing and the thing stood for may be familiar or conventional—*the grave* for death, *heart* for love or the affections—or it may be created within the context of a particular story, as with Hulga's artificial leg in Flannery O'Connor's story "Good Country People" or the "hills like white elephants" in Hemingway's story by that name. Metonyms created within stories stay in the mind not because what they stand for is straightforward but because in the telling they come to have emotional complexity.

In the words of Flannery O'Connor, fiction is an incarnational art. Its material is not concepts but the flesh and blood and dirt and dust of the physical world. Fiction portrays a cleaning woman riding home on a bus after being fired by her employer for a theft she didn't commit, not by language directly describing her emotional state *(angry, hurt, bitter)* but by an accumulation of metonymic details of behavior, perceptions, and thoughts: her compulsive throat clearing, say, or an incident of casual cruelty or racism elsewhere on the bus. This is what enables readers to discover for themselves what's going on for this woman. The author who puts a label on the woman's emotions has short-circuited the process of emotional understanding that fiction is about.

Perhaps the most common general problem in student stories is the failure to enter into the minds of characters and into the particulars of their experience. It's easier to proceed shallowly—i.e., conceptually—to hew a path closer to what we consciously intend our story to mean. It's far easier for an author to "sit on" the story in this way and not allow the characters to have their own lives. But just as characters in literary fiction are not sociological types, fiction is not about abstractions but about depicting particular, distinctive people in particular, distinctive situations. It's through the emotional truth of these depictions, not the generalizing movement of abstraction, that the best literary fiction achieves its universality. The hard work for the author is discovering just what the lives of his characters are actually about, because in order to enter into their minds with accuracy and truth, he needs to be in touch with his own emotional realities. This can mean slow, messy, confusing, sometimes painful work. But it's the necessary work of literary fiction, because only by mining personal realities can an author come up with the metonymic material necessary to carry the emotional weight of the story. Without true, emotional detail—without metonymy—no story can live and breathe.

▪▫▪ THE EXERCISE ▪▪▫▪▪▪▪▪▪▪▪▪▪▪▪▪▪▪▪▫▪▪▪▪▪▫▪▪▪▪▪▪▪▫▪▫

Take forty-five minutes to write a scene, with or without dialogue
(but not *all* in dialogue), in which one member of a couple
returns home with a gift, a find, or a purchase that is somehow
off, or wrong, either in itself, in the timing, or in terms of the
relationship more generally. It could be a banal or trivial thing:
he's come back from the store with the wrong shower curtain
hooks. Or she's bought an enormous ceramic head. Or he rescues
a bird stunned by flying into their windowpane. Whatever it is,
the reader should finish the scene with an insight into the nature
of the relationship between these two people and a sense that
something within it has either just inexorably changed or been
newly revealed.

In this exercise, the thing that is brought back operates as a
metonym, a primary means by which the scene embodies the
off-ness of the relationship. Writers tackling this exercise should
bear in mind that readers are savvy when it comes to relationships in drama and fiction and highly sensitive to where small
moments within them are likely pointing. From the artistic
point of view, this is both a disadvantage and an advantage.
The disadvantage is that because this is extremely familiar,
well-trodden ground, it can be a challenge to be original. (But
personal experience will be a richer metonymic source than
imagination. It's easier to be original when drawing honestly
from experience.) The advantage is that the wiser readers are
to a certain dramatic situation, the greater subtlety and indirectness the writer can employ for her effects, because her readers
will readily pick up on the smallest hints. Every reader enjoys
the illusion of being the only one on the inside track of what is
really going on for the characters in a story. Metonymy—in
which the connection of the thing to what is going on is

unstated yet emotionally true—is the fictional device *par excellence* for providing each and every reader with that feeling.

SUGGESTED READING

The short story writer Raymond Carver is a modern master of metonymy. Consider the peacock in the story "Feathers" in Carver's collection *Cathedral*. This bird is no conventional symbol of pride or vanity, but what the narrator and his wife blame, along with its owners' "ugly baby," for their entire life going wrong—and what is that about? What does the narrative context in which Carver places the baby and the peacock, and what does the kind of language he uses to convey the narrator's view of them, tell us about the narrator and his relationship to his wife and friends and subsequently to his "conniving" son? Embodied in that baby and that peacock is an emotionally charged mystery that is the stuff of fiction.

In the title story of the collection, a blind man convinces the narrator to help him "see" a cathedral by allowing him to ride the narrator's hand with his own while the narrator draws one. For the narrator, that moment is "like nothing else in my life up to now," and, reading the story, we sense how this truly could be the case. That image of the blind man's hand riding the narrator's is a dramatic, metonymic image that carries the power of the significance for the narrator and for us, without anything being told to anybody.

One story "Preservation," in *Cathedral*, is a metonymic tour de force. A wife comes home to find that her depressed husband has failed to notice the fridge has broken down. To prevent the pork chops from spoiling, she cooks them and places one on his plate. To her, "the meat didn't look like meat. It looked like part of an old shoulder blade, or a digging instrument." Here Carver actually dramatizes the mystery inherent in the metonym. The character cannot recognize the pork chop for what it is. Instead, she, like the reader, experiences its metonymic force. It's as if she were trying to read the pork chop the way we read a story, except that to her its meaning seems inappropriate. (How inappropriate it is for us, is up to us.) This is a remarkable moment, and yet, less than a page later, Carver has the boldness and skill to do it again. The water from the melted icebox has pooled on the kitchen floor. The husband is barefoot: "She stared down at her husband's bare feet. She stared at his feet next to the pool of water. She knew she'd never again in her life see anything so unusual." All the strangeness, fear, and uncertainty being experienced by this woman in response to her husband's breakdown is embodied in that mysterious, baffling image of her husband's bare feet in the meltwater. Naming the woman's emotions in this situation would be a bloodless, typifying, almost—in the context of such a story—insulting (to us, to the woman) act. Instead we are given a metonym with strange and powerful effect. A few more lines—in which Carver stays with the husband's feet through the eyes of his wife—and the story ends.

Advice

A metonym gets its strength from its rightness for the story. Sometimes an image will be the germ for a story and remain at its metaphoric heart. Sometimes after giving rise to a story, it will need to be cut. Sometimes you won't know what the necessary metonyms for a story are until well into the writing of it. Sometimes when a metonym in a story feels as though it's being made to work too hard it will be because the author isn't quite sure yet what the story is about.

Tip for New Writers

If you want to write, you need to know that the greatest reward is almost certainly going to be the pleasure of doing it. Either you write because you need to, or you write for the love of it. If you write only for the satisfaction of having written, for the pride of publication, or for the cachet of being a writer, then you're a consumer of a manufactured good, not an artist.

WHAT'S LEFT UNSAID: THE IMPORTANCE OF SUBTEXT
Alix Ohlin

We're often told to write what we know and, when it comes to dialogue, what we hear. Indeed, it's absolutely true that an ear for the sounds and stutters and slang of everyday speech brings characters to life, and that skateboarding teenagers in California should sound different on the page from elderly accountants in Toronto. But it's equally important to pay attention, in writing dialogue, to what's left unsaid: the subtext lurking beneath the sounds and stutters and slang.

Real-life conversations are full of subtext. That guy at the office who won't stop boasting about his Friday night bowling league championship is really insisting that he isn't the loser everyone else thinks he is. That girl in the food court at the mall flipping her hair and laughing really hard at her friend's joke is really telling the boy who works at Chik Fil-A that she thinks he's cute. Body language, gestures, and the dropped cues in speech itself all serve to betray a person's secret mission.

Subtext in dialogue rings true, then, and it also helps modu-late tone: if you had all your characters coming right out and saying what they meant ("I love you, Dad, but I'm under too much pressure to meet the high expectations you set because of your own past failures"), you'd wind up with a parade of absurdly overemotional speeches akin to the scenery-chewing clips they show at the Oscars.

But it's not for realism's sake that subtext matters. (After all, realism itself is an artifice; if we wrote *truly* realistic dialogue, our characters would deliver long speeches full of *ums* and *ahs* and descriptions of the tuna salad they ate for lunch.) Rather, it matters because it deepens the tension and complexity of a story. Ultimately, subtext is important not because people don't usually say what they want, but because people don't usually *know* what they want, much less what others want. The shifting sands of this knowledge and the partial articulation of these desires are part of what makes life, and fiction, mysterious—and every good story is a mystery story, broadly defined.

Considering subtext, then, is a way of playing with the intrigu-ing and imperfect and dynamic levels of knowledge in any piece of fiction: what does each character know about him or herself, about the other characters, and what does the reader know? At what point, if any, will the subtext rise up and break the surface of the dialogue? What's left unsaid by the characters is often the place where their lives are most tellingly revealed.

■■■ THE EXERCISE ■■■■■■■■■■■■■■■■■■■■■■■■■■■■■■■■■

This exercise is in two parts.

 1. Go to a coffee shop, restaurant, bar, etc., and observe two people having a conversation. Sit close enough that you can

hear what they're saying (but far enough away that they won't notice you and become self-conscious). Take notes on what they're actually saying for a while. Then stop transcribing the dialogue and take notes, instead, on everything else: their body language, their gestures, the space between them. Who's leaning forward and who's sitting back? Who pays the check and after how much negotiation? Write down what you think the subtext of their conversation is. Then look back at the dialogue you transcribed and examine it for the dropped hints that reveal the correlation between what's been said and what hasn't.

2. Now that your awareness of subtext has been heightened, write a scene with two characters. Over the course of the scene, one character must tell the other "I love you"—but not in so many words. (No synonyms or euphemisms, either.) Make the profession of love take place in the subtext. The other character doesn't feel the same way; this takes place in the subtext, too. Bear in mind that this doesn't have to be a love scene between a couple—it can take place just as easily between a parent and a child, two friends, co-workers, etc. Whether or not the subtext is clear to each character, and to what degree, is your decision, but it should be clear to the reader by the end of the scene where each character stands.

SUGGESTED READING

In Edith Wharton's *The Age of Innocence*, the characters converse almost entirely in a devastatingly polite, highly mannered tone about opera performances and European vacations, beneath which placid surface the passions of their lives course ferociously. It is a code that everyone in a certain sphere of society can understand. Wharton brilliantly manipulates the subtext of these conversations to comment on the stultifying conformity of her characters' lives. Newland Archer, the hero of the novel, fancies himself a free thinker, capable of both participating in yet mocking these social mores, until he meets Ellen Olenska, his fiancée (and then wife) and May's cousin, who represents everything that is truly free. Her greatest unconventionality is that she says what she thinks.

Newland falls in love with Ellen and plans to leave May and New York for her. At the climactic moment of the book, May informs him that she's pregnant, thereby making his escape impossible. Her confession of the news is partial and coded, as blushingly indirect as a woman of her time is supposed to be: *"For you see, Newland, I've been sure since this morning of something I've been so longing and hoping for—"* "Oh, my dear," *he said, holding her to him while his cold hand stroked her hair.*

What's masterful in this sentence is the fact that Newland understands what May means immediately. In response he mutters the poignantly ambiguous phrase, "Oh, my dear," while his body language reveals his heartbroken, conflicted self: a man who knows to stroke his wife's hair, yet whose hand is cold.

Newland thinks that he is the first to hear the news. But May goes on to tell him that she'd told Ellen she was pregnant two weeks before she actually knew it, therefore sending her rival away forever. She also tells him why: *Her color burned deeper, but she held his gaze.* "No, I wasn't sure then—but I told her I was. And you see I was right!" *she exclaimed, her blue eyes wet with victory.*

In the subtext of this dialogue, May's character stands truly revealed—not as the blindly conformist innocent Newland took her for but as a steely woman whose conventionality is part and parcel of her strength. And she and Newland understand one another perfectly, which is to say that they are bound together against outsiders such as Ellen. The balance of power between Newland and May shifts forever in this scene, the fates of three people are decided, and all of it happens beneath the surface of a happy bride bringing her husband some good news.

Advice

As is clear from discussing this scene of Wharton's, subtext can't be properly used without a full understanding of character, deployed at the correct moment for maximum effect. You can't write subtext if you aren't sure what's going on in the darkest recesses of the characters' minds. You have to know more than they do. Practicing social observation and the writing of subtext is way of cultivating that understanding on the part of the writer. And, of course, the fun of the exercise is that it allows you to indulge in eavesdropping on other people, then gossiping about their motives, all for the sake of art.

INTERVIEW
Val McDermid

What's your strategy for blocking out the world while you write?

I play music. What kind of music depends on the book and where I am in the process. It can be anything from Mozart to Pat Metheny, Mary Gauthier to Radiohead.

What is your process of writing a book, from start to finish?

A complicated answer, because my process has changed dramatically lately. I think most writers use their first two or three books to figure out what method of writing works best for them. I wrote *Report for Murder* more or less by the seat of my pants. I didn't know where it was heading or how it was going to get there. I wasted a lot of time writing myself into blind alleys and trying to shoehorn characters into unlikely behavior. With the second book, *Common Murder,* I thought it might help to have a better idea of where I was going. So I wrote a brief outline. Just a couple of scribbled pages. But it made life so much easier. I felt freed by its presence, as if it were a talisman that would keep me on the straight and narrow. By the third book, I was writing a ten-page chapter-by-chapter breakdown. It worked for me. It was like a roadmap, and having it allowed me to drive off in any direction that took my fancy because I always knew where I was heading for to get back on to the story spine. And that is pretty much how it stayed until *The Torment of Others*.

Now, I have always maintained that writing is a process in which we never arrive at the destination. Every book is a challenge to do better or to do different than before. Every book is an opportunity to learn the mistakes of the past (and of other writers!) and to push harder at the limits of one's capabilities. So I've always been open to the possibility of change and development. I just didn't think it was going to come at the expense of everything I thought I knew about method.

It started two books back with *The Torment of Others* and it felt like a serious problem. Everything up to the point where I was about to start writing had gone as usual in my head. I'd taken the story from first starburst of idea to something that had a bit of shape. I knew whose story it was and how they got to where they were at the start of the book. I could hear their voices in my head, and I thought I was ready to roll. I started working on the synopsis, and the beginning went as usual. I had the outline of the eighty or so pages neatly in place. And that's when the trouble started. I couldn't articulate what happened next. There was a vague, amorphous shape in my head, but I couldn't grasp it. I wrestled with this for a while, then decided to leave it alone, on the general principle that my subconscious would have it sorted when I went back to it. I did some work on the end of the book, trying to make clear where I was headed, to see if that would help me figure out how I was going to get there. And the ending seemed to come together quite readily. At least now I knew what I was aiming for. I went back to the synopsis. And still it wouldn't come together. By now, my deadline was looming and I had no alternative but to buckle down and write the damn book. I just got my head down and wrote straight through, barely pausing to sleep and eat. It was physically draining and mentally exhausting. And ironically, my editor maintained this was the strongest first draft I'd ever handed in.

I thought it was just a glitch. A one-off. That when I got immersed in the next book, *The Grave Tattoo*, everything would be as it was before. After all, I'd been building this book in my head for years, doing the research, figuring out the story. And I did have a reasonable idea of the story. But this time it was worse. I couldn't even get the beginning or the end down. I knew more or less where

I was going, but I couldn't pin down the kind of detail that would let me draw my map. It was a nightmare. I really was beginning to wonder if I had lost it. If I had come to the end of the road as a writer. But again, the deadline was looming and so I tried to get the book down. It felt like walking out on a high wire without a safety net. And the first time, I fell off. I got about fifty pages in and I panicked. I would sit for hours staring at the screen, trying all the tricks I knew to kick-start myself. But nothing worked. I crashed the first deadline with embarrassing aplomb. I'd never been late before, had been scathing about the irresponsibility of authors who messed everyone by not delivering on time, and here I was, being scathed by my own words.

I was so embarrassed about the whole thing, I pretended it just wasn't happening. I was nonchalant when asked about the book, insouciant about its potential delivery date. It was awful. I wasn't sleeping properly, I was avoiding other writers, and I felt like a fraud.

It was desperation in the end that got me moving. I couldn't go on pretending to write the damn thing forever. I forced myself to my desk and made myself do it. And as I did that, something shifted. I realized there was another way of doing this crazy thing that was working for me now. It's what I later discovered the American writer E.L. Doctorow calls "driving at night writing." Imagine you're setting off at night to drive somewhere. You know where you are heading, you know the way there. But you can only see a small part of the road lit up ahead of you. And as you drive forward, the road reveals itself piece by piece until you finally reach your destination. And that is the kind of writer I seem to have become. I've since written a novella and I'm working on my new book, both by this method. I am now, it appears, a night driver.

What's important to you about setting? About character?

Setting plays an important role, partly because it creates a picture in the reader's head. I think it's particularly important in crime fiction because it helps to create the suspension of disbelief. Deep down, we all know crimes are not solved in the way we describe, so we need to give readers all the help we can so they can become immersed in the journey we're taking them on. If the setting is powerful and accurate, readers are more inclined to believe we're telling them the truth about the other stuff.

Character is what makes a story worth pursuing. Otherwise, it's like a board game. The crime novel is often accused of being plot-driven, but I think it's at its best when the characters are as important as the plot. The crime novel is a great way to write about people in extremis, which is when, of course, their true natures stand exposed.

What are you most proud of as far as your writing style/craft?

That I have grown and developed so much from my early beginnings as a writer.

What would you like to improve on craft-wise, if anything?

I'm always looking for interesting structural ways to tell a story rather than the directly linear approach.

What personality traits define you as a writer?

A rich fantasy life, a certain tenacity, and enough of the Protestant work ethic to make sure the books get written.

What's the hardest part of writing for you?

Getting started. Once I have a rhythm going, it's comfortable. But getting to that point is excruciatingly hard work.

How do you feel about book readings, and what have you learned is important when reading your work out loud to an audience?

Always ask the organizer what the audience is expecting. If they want 45 minutes, they're going to be brassed off if you only read for 15. The other key thing is to practice in advance and mark the text up so you can give the words their maximum movement. I enjoy reading and try to choose passages that are lively and don't need much explanation.

How much and what sorts of things do you read?

I read crime fiction and literary fiction mostly, with a little poetry on the side. I only really read nonfiction when it's relevant to an idea I'm working on or toying with. I also read newspapers, blogs, and magazine articles online. What I'm always interested in is good writing, wherever I find it. I generally read two to three books a week.

If the writing life is a pie, how would you slice it up, and what size would the pieces be?

35% talent, 40% hard work, 25% luck.

What have you sacrificed to be a writer and is it worth it?

I don't think I've sacrificed anything of significance. I had a couple of financially tough years when I started writing full time, when I gave up drink and buying books and music. Doing without decent wine was hard, but the library filled the gap for the other stuff.

What gets you in the mood to write?

Fear of my editor. Guilt at the amount of time I've been spending reading, playing guitar, and computer games.

You have stories brewing in your head for years sometimes. How do you know when it's time to get writing?

I don't know. I just do. It feels ripe, somehow.

Do you think the subconscious plays a role in writing?

A huge role. This is the only job (apart from being a sleep-research guinea pig) in which you can work while you're asleep. I've lost count of the number of times I've gone to sleep running through the questions I need to resolve before the next day's writing. Nine times out of ten, the answers are there in the shower the next morning.

I think when writers say that fatuous thing about "the characters just took on a life of their own," what they are doing is taking the credit away from their subconscious. Of course characters don't have minds of their own. The only agency they have is that which we give them. When they appear to take a different path from the one we had originally mapped out for them, that's the subconscious grabbing the wheel and driving them in the right direction.

What are the low points of being a writer? What are the high points?

The low points are

1. The bad days when the words are intractable and it all feels like complete and utter crap.

2. Sleepless nights in strange beds in hotel rooms in unfamiliar cities on book tours where your face hurts from smiling.

The highest point is when someone praises your work in terms that tell you they've really understood what you were trying to do.

Will you always write?

I hope so. I can't imagine life without it.

THE FOUND STORY

Marnie Woodrow

Getting to the desk is half the battle in a writing life, and it's also important to retain a sense of play as you work, or why bother? Ninety-nine percent of writers aren't in it for the money—that would be folly. We may be a little masochistic as we watch a million sunny days fly past outside the office window, but we're doing what we love, and that's what matters. Which isn't to say it's always going to go well every day. Whenever the sap isn't flowing as fast as I'd like on a piece of writing, I employ the found story technique. Chances are, my more domineering passion for my current project will kick in, and I'll abandon the exercise for the decidedly more fascinating kingdom of my novel or short story du jour. In any case, this exercise is loads of fun and yields really interesting results. I love to be surprised; it's why I write.

THE EXERCISE

This exercise requires a few supplementary "texts" and a sense of fun. If you find yourself unable to access an idea out of thin air, this can be a good jump-start technique.

Open a white pages phone directory to a random page and let your eye fall on the middle listings. Choose a name that catches your eye and write it down. Close the phone book and then open it again, randomly. Write down the name that appears at the bottom of the right-hand page. If only initials are shown, create a first name for these two people.

Next, open a world atlas or unfold a roadmap and close your eyes. *Drop your finger down and then open your eyes:* this is the location of the story you are about to write.

Open the dictionary to a random page. *Study the first three word definitions featured on the left-hand page.* Write down the words. These words will somehow inform the plot or theme of your new story. If the words really don't inspire you, close the dictionary and try again once more. Being picky defeats the purpose.

Using these points of reference, create a five- to ten-page short story that uses the found names, location, and plot/theme directives. Write a first draft as fast as possible, without worrying if you know anything at all about the cultures of the characters as suggested by their names, and without worrying about authentic setting details for the found location. Focus on the mystery of the people, place, and what they are facing/experiencing.

When revising the new story, use Google or another internet search engine to help you gain greater authority regarding character culture and the setting. Be careful to cross-reference if sending this story out into the world: the internet isn't always a reliable source of information.

SUGGESTED READING

I think every writer should read John Dos Passos's novel *Manhattan Transfer*, first published in 1925. It demonstrates a sense of play, control, and courage and has a huge cast of characters who stamp in and out of the frame, fending off their loneliness with admirable ingenuity. While the language may sometimes sound mannered to our contemporary ears, to me it possesses a snap reminiscent of the best old movies from the 1930s and 1940s. Dos Passos also experimented with two techniques: newsreel (using headlines and snippets of news from newspapers) and the camera's eye (letting the reader see events unfold that one of the main characters could not have attended, such as a court case much in the news or some other closed event).

Advice

Stop thinking about getting published, which is the opposite energy of play. There's an anxious energy when we start worrying about "career" that isn't conducive to spirited writing. Enjoy the process, from the sound of the keyboard clacking to the suspension of your own disbelief as you go along. Go out on limbs, take chances, mix things up.

THE INSTANT STORY

Marnie Woodrow

There's something about being bossed around that helps a writer get down to writing. It's also helpful to imagine the basic elements that drive a story: a sense of something happening, a turning point, a resolution, however traumatic for the characters. In an instant story, you don't have time to mess around: the first, middle, and last sentences are there and you've only got one page in which to tell a compelling tale. I strongly encourage writers to do this exercise more than once, using the same first, middle, and final lines to push the possibilities in new directions.

▪▪▪ THE EXERCISE ▪▪▪▪▪▪▪▪▪▪▪▪▪▪▪▪▪▪▪▪▪▪▪▪▪▪▪▪▪▪▪▪▪▪▪▪▪

On a fresh sheet of paper, write the following:

Last line first, bottom of the page: *Not everyone can be so wise so young.*

Middle of the page: *Marjory's face began to turn blue.*

First line, top of page: A line you personally think it would be fun to scream in a public place, or something you've always wanted to say to someone who gets under your skin.

Now choose an environment where multiple characters would gather and cross paths. Have fun with whether or not the characters involved know each other, or whether it's a story about strangers and their impact on one another. Example environments are sporting events, conventions, train stations/airports, waiting rooms, book clubs or self-help meetings, etc. By doing this exercise over and over, you'll flex muscles of all kinds. One draft may have a comic tone, another may be a dark tragedy.

Beginning with the first line, write down to the middle of the page, then incorporate the line *Marjory's face began to turn blue,* and continue writing down to the last line, trying to write as sensibly as possible but without worrying about being perfect.

SUGGESTED READING

I'm an ardent fan of Patricia Highsmith, most famous for her Ripley novels. Her stories and novels crackle with tension, and that's something you can learn through writing one-page stories. Zero in and hit the conflict immediately. That's what the reader cares about: what's going to happen? One of my favorite Highsmith novels is *Strangers on a Train.* Two people meet someplace typical (aboard a train, as the title cleverly suggests), yet there will be nothing typical about their collision. Highsmith wasn't one to wax on, either, and her spare style is a lesson to us all. Besides, you can almost hear her cackling from the Great Desk Beyond about all the grief she caused her characters.

Advice

No matter what type of fiction you're writing, read thrillers and watch movies that have a suspenseful element. Pacing and driving a plot along is a skill any writer can apply to his or her work, no matter what the genre. Keep things happening, keep the pages turning through evocative language and character, as well as through *pacing*. The highest compliment a writer can receive is, "I was up all night reading your book."

FiVE TiPS

Frances Itani

1. **Trust your voice.** Let your voice out. This might be one of the most difficult things to learn, but a writer often learns it in the early stages of apprenticeship. Read aloud, especially your later drafts. This is your voice. This is your unique rhythm, the pulse and breath of your words. This is the sound of you as a writer. Trust that voice.

2. **Don't rob your reader.** I like to leave plenty of room for the reader to enter and experience the story. This means exercising restraint. It also means being ruthless when you are working on final drafts. A writer is a storyteller, yes, but a storyteller who invites the reader inside, not one who holds the reader outside of the work. This can be done in a number of ways: don't overexplain; write for your most intelligent reader; trust that, yes, the reader will understand what you are doing and will meet you halfway. If you do your work well and present your ideas in a concrete way through story, character, image, and sensuous detail, your reader will become your partner and will do the abstracting. As you write more and more, you will learn what to leave in and

what to leave out. And try not to judge your characters. Judging is another way of robbing the reader. "Only present," Chekhov wrote. Believe me, a reader is perfectly capable of making up his or her mind about how he or she feels about a character.

3. **"Go where it grabs you the most!"** The late W.O. Mitchell, novelist, teacher, former mentor, and dear friend, said those words to me one day when I asked how he approached an immense canvas such as a novel-in-progress. How do you choose what you will work on each day?

   It seems simple enough, but when you get up in the morning and are faced with hundreds of pages of draft material, or freefall, or research, and when you are working with many ideas, many chapters, many sections that have to be pieced together seamlessly, well, Go where it grabs you the most! This has been one of the best pieces of advice I've ever been given. As an extension of this, I will also say: allow surprises in your work. Work organically, so that the material grows out of itself, without you imposing rigid structure, such as predesigned plot or fixed content. When your work surprises you, accept this with delight, not resistance. Leave the doors wide open for change, even change in the direction of thematic intent.

4. **Learn when not to write.** Because I was raising two babies when I first began to write fiction, I used to experience intense frustration when I could not get near the blank page every day. I was a university student during the same period, which meant that every minute, every hour had to be carefully apportioned. It took a while, but I learned that when I could not work on my stories because of other responsibilities, it was better to stay away and not even try. That way,

there was no frustration. Instead, I learned to create a healthy tension between me and the work being held off. A few days later, or a week later, when I could see a longer stretch of time ahead, I was able to re-enter my story in a better state of mind.

Another way of dealing with this kind of frustration—not being able to get near one's own work—is to continue reading during these periods. I always read in bank and grocery-store lineups, in waiting rooms, in coffee shops. I leave a paperback in the car at all times so that I will never be without a book. One can use this non-writing time to learn how other writers solve problems of structure or point of view, for instance. It's all part of the same (never-ending) apprenticeship. For me, reading and writing demand different spaces. I can read with people around me, but I can't write. Many writers who have young families face the conditions I have described. The ideal situation is to write every day, but if you cannot, I repeat, learn when not to write. It's better than getting ulcers.

5. **Back to trust again: Trust your intuition, and let your subconscious do its work.** While you are consciously at work on a book—story, novel, poem, play, essay—another part of your brain is engaged, like a secret, subterranean part of yourself. This can often be the problem-solving part, the part that suggests connection and resonance. I find that after (not before) I write for several hours, a long walk, a tai chi or lok hup set, a workout in the gym, or going to a film alone helps to set the conscious mind aside and let ideas below the surface simmer and move about. I have often found my endings this way. While the work is simmering, and while I am engaged in another activity, the

final scene of a story or novel might appear like a gift, an inevitability.

You can't force this to happen, but you can help to create the conditions.

ANIMATE A THREE-DIMENSIONAL WORLD

Catherine Bush

When we think about introducing movement into our prose, we tend to think of the need to describe characters in action, and the importance of employing strong and lively verbs to do so. All well and good. But while a character may be active, pacing the corridor of her apartment, driven by a desire to forget her bad day at the toothpaste factory, spearing a glass from an upper shelf and, finding no absinthe in the cupboard, banging out the door, she may still be moving through two-dimensional space, a largely flat world. Now it's time to animate your fictional world as a three-dimensional environment with three-dimensional people moving through it. (We tend to think of three-dimensionality as a psychological state that we want our characters to achieve, but it's also a physical one. We want readers to imagine our characters, and their environments, as having literal solidity and depth.)

Think of ways in which you can create a sense of volume, depth, and solidity for the reader. Shifts in visual perspective—

moving the reader's eye and attention from high to low, from near to far—can help provide a sense of depth. Oddly, something glimpsed through something else, or the image of something frail or translucent moving over something more solid, can heighten the sense of the latter's solidity. The wavery image of a child's magic lantern circling the walls of a bedroom can make the walls themselves feel more dense, more present in the reader's mind. Rain drumming on a bare arm, a shadow darting along a woman's neck can make the body feel more corporeal. The movement of cloth—the sharp twist of a shirt, cotton pulling at the underarms, or the billow of a dress as a woman reaches for a penny fallen to the floor—can not only accentuate the movement but suggest the volume of the body beneath the clothing.

THE EXERCISE

Describe a character moving from an exterior landscape to an interior one in search of something. Pay particular attention to the ways in which you can enhance a sense of three-dimensionality—volume, depth, and solidity—in the fictional world. Keep in mind that a convincingly imagined world is also an animate one, a world experienced with depth *and* in motion.

SUGGESTED READING

While not a how-to writing guide by any means, *Dreaming by the Book,* by philosopher and critic Elaine Scarry, offers a fascinating analysis of what our minds do when we read fiction, how we create vivid imaginary worlds in our heads, and how writers induce us to do so. As Scarry herself notes, Flaubert, in *Madame Bovary,* is a genius at moving the human body beneath cloth and using the movement of cloth to suggest the volume, the corporeality, of the body beneath.

Advice

Remember that on one level your writing is a series of instructions to the reader: Imagine this, then this, then this. You want the experience of imagining your fictional world to be an active and vivid one. Interesting instructions will help make your fictional world convincing and immersive, not so much like a dream as like the actual experiencing of another world.

OBSERVATION AS A STATE OF MIND

Catherine Bush

You feel like you're always calling attention to the same sorts of details (light bouncing off car windows, off any window). Characters always seem to be observed performing the same sorts of gestures (blinking or tugging their hair when nervous). Your fictional world feels a bit generic, physically and psychically dull. What to do? You may think you need to be searching for originality when what you really need is to dive even more deeply into your chosen point of view. Whether you're telling your story using a first person perspective or third (or second) doesn't matter. Truly inhabiting a point of view means more than getting behind a character's eyes or inhabiting his or her voice. Getting inside someone's head isn't simply about having access to thoughts or emotional states, either. Character also shapes observation at every turn. The personality of your point-of-view character fundamentally affects how she takes in the world. And a character's current state of mind just as crucially affects what she observes.

A mapmaker walking through a city may see its buildings in terms of lines and measurements, noticing every true and wonky angle. A mapmaker with a migraine will feel every pulsing line and jagged angle pressing in on her. A man whose wife has just run off on him in a little red car will walk through the streets noticing something else again (red cars everywhere), just as a pregnant woman walking into a supermarket will pick up on very different details than a woman whose lover is dying. Different kinds of people (a podiatrist, a mathematics professor) will notice different things about other people, too.

▪▪▪ THE EXERCISE ▪▪▪▪▪▪▪▪▪▪▪▪▪▪▪▪▪▪▪▪▪▪▪▪▪▪▪▪▪▪

1. Walk down a street that's familiar to you in the guise of one of your characters (this can also be a way of opening up a character if you're feeling stuck). Think not only about what sort of person she is but the state of mind she is in when your story opens, or in the particular scene that you're working on (what's bothering her, preoccupying her, obsessing her, distracting her). What details of her surroundings will she observe? Take notes. Do this same exercise with another character (again, pay attention not only to personality, and how this affects what she or he observes, but the state of mind).

2. Write a description of a supermarket from the point of view of someone in love. Describe the same place from the point of view of someone whose mother is dying.

3. Write a scene at a party from two points of view: someone in love on the lookout for his or her lover and someone who's just quit smoking.

SUGGESTED READING

In her novel *Paradise,* Scottish writer A.L. Kennedy does a superb job of being deeply inside the head of her protagonist, Hannah Luckraft, an alcoholic. What Kennedy seems most interested in is not the sociology of alcoholism but alcoholism as a state of mind and a state of perception; among many other things, the novel is a tour de force of skewed observation rendered in sharp, unusual sentences.

Advice

Remember that what people fail to notice can be as revelatory as what they do observe. Every act of observation is an act of selection, choosing one detail while leaving others out. The personality of your character, and her state of mind, will help determine these acts of selection.

FOR WORKSHOPS
AND
WRITING GROUPS

THE WAR AGAINST CLICHÉ

Andrew Pyper

Clichés are unavoidable. Even the most innovative prose stylists fall prey to the lazy image or off-the-rack turn of phrase from time to time. If a novel were composed entirely free of description we have seen somewhere else before, it would unquestionably be a work of genius, but likely unreadable. It would be *Finnegans Wake.*

To make this concession to the pervasiveness of convention is not the same thing, however, as permitting it free rein in one's writing. One must still resist the temptation of raging sunsets and babbling brooks, for, as Martin Amis has put it, the writer who achieves a truly individual prose style is one who is most fiercely engaged in the war against cliché.

Most of the time, the threat of tired description comes not from a lack of talent (and is thus irreparable) but from lack of work. The lure of cliché is its convenience: plop in the word you've seen next to the words around it a thousand times and you're that much closer to the next page. But cheaters always get caught in the end. In a workshop setting, when participants read aloud from their work, you can see the blushing that results when they confront their own laziness. What looked acceptable amid the blur of ink on the page announces its own death when released into the air.

How to Use This Exercise to Get Out of Giving a Speech

In the past, in the middle of talks I have been invited to give on "the writing life" or some such topic, I have instead given the audience an instant exercise. Why listen to me when you can begin your own fantastic writing career right now, from that foldout chair you're sitting in, scribbling on the back of a receipt?

I tell people to imagine a tomato. Not any tomato, mind you, not a tomato as you might see it painted in a child's book meant to teach the child to point at the picture and say, "Tomato!" but a tomato you have known intimately in your life. A tomato you have touched, unintentionally bruised, selected for purchase, or slipped in your pocket, guiltily, as you passed the grocer's stand at the outdoor market. Before writing a word, stop to really *think* about this tomato for at least a full minute. Turn it about in your hands. Note how, like a snowflake, no other tomato known to history is precisely the same as *your* tomato.

Then I ask the audience members to write a description of their tomatoes. After three minutes, the bravest souls are invited to stand and read their pieces. In many instances, the very first reader falls into the trap. That is, he or she uses one or all of the words *red, plump,* or *juicy.* That's when I shout a good-humored *"A-ha!"* because these are words that belong to the generic tomato, the child's book tomato, and not the one and only tomato in your mind. What this trap illustrates is the injustice you are doing your tomato by not going to the trouble of giving it an individual identity.

∎∎∎ THE EXERCISE ∎∎∎∎∎∎∎∎∎∎∎∎∎∎∎∎∎∎∎∎∎∎∎∎∎∎∎∎∎∎∎∎∎∎

In a more formal workshop setting, I like to use this same kind of exercise in a series, encouraging the participants to not only free themselves from the obvious but to get wilder and wilder—and often more wonderfully particular—in the way they work around the constraints the exercise puts on them.

The idea here is to teach ourselves to stop and think about how something looks or feels or smells, and to take the time to work out a precise—and novel—way of putting it into words. In short, this exercise reminds us of the labor involved in producing fresh prose, as well as the necessary risk.

Below are a handful of examples I have used in the past, but any number of similarly constructed tasks could be used. The point of the exercise can be even more forcefully made if each assignment is done on the spot, with time limits imposed for both the *envisioning* front end and the *writing* back end. I usually don't allow pen to touch paper for a full minute, then give three or four minutes to write the description. The result needn't be long. One fresh phrase can, when read aloud, elicit sighs of recognition and envy from fellow participants … as well as from the instructor.

1. Describe an obese person without using any word appearing under *fat* in a thesaurus.

2. Describe the sky without using *blue* (or any of its variants), *clouds,* or *sun.*

3. To claim intimate knowledge of a thing, people often say *I know it like the back of my hand.* But how well do we really know the backs of our own hands? Describe the back of your hand without any mention of its literal, anatomical properties, i.e., veins, wrinkles, knuckles, etc.

4. Describe a sound someone makes that, through its description alone (that is, without directly naming it), we can identify as laughter.

SUGGESTED READING

I mentioned Martin Amis as a writer who is a leader in the war against cliché (in fact, this is the title of one of his collections of criticism). He happens also to be someone who, in this respect, practices what he preaches. I know of no other contemporary novelist whose books provide the open-it-anywhere pleasure of Amis. My day is often stalled by pulling *Money* or *London Fields* randomly open and reading a paragraph describing the precise torments of a character's hangover or the depressing interior of the pub in which the same hangover was paid for. These midday, mid-book visitations invariably end in snorts of laughter.

What I love about Amis's writing is the lengths he goes to in order to render his seedy, cigarette-addicted, greedy, booze-addled world afresh. It is this effort that can lead to establishing what usually goes by the name of a writer's "voice." When you're reading Amis, you know you're reading Amis, for better or worse.

By way of illustration, pick up any of his novels and, if you haven't the time to read the whole thing, read whatever happens to be on page 147 of the edition in your hands. I guarantee there will be something described there that makes it new.

As for a specific recommendation, why not start with *The Information*. It's one of his best (and most underrated) novels, I think, and contains the most hilarious drunken-awakenings-in-unfamiliar-surroundings I've ever read.

TRANSLATING STYLES
James Wilcox

In the 1950s, Ernst von Dohnanyi, a Hungarian composer whom Brahms had praised, was teaching at Florida State University. My father, a doctoral student with a wife and four children, had to write a four-part fugue for his final exam in Dohnanyi's composition class. At this time, our family was crammed into student housing, a cement-block cottage that seemed like a mansion to me. I was very compact then and showed signs of being interested in candy. As for this baroque fugue that had to be in E flat minor, I could've cared less. Yes, Dad had to contend with six flats, mixing it up with those four unruly voices—and he hadn't the slightest sympathy from this son. In any case, Dad nonetheless managed to harmonize the different strains and get his degree.

Much later, as an assistant editor at Random House, this same son learned something about different strains from a non-Hungarian mentor. Dr. Hunter S. Thompson told me that he used to type out pages from various classic authors such as Hemingway or Henry James. He wanted to pound out their words so he could feel the shape and heft of their sentences. Thompson's editor at Random House had asked me to help out with his manuscript when Thompson came to town. As a closet writer burning with a furtive ambition, I never forgot any advice Dr. Thompson tossed my way. Nor did I forget the dinner we had one evening at a Mexican restaurant. Just before dessert, a flame emerged from Hunter's mouth accompanied by a shriek from the director of publicity—an E flat two octaves above middle C. Hunter later explained that he had dribbled lighter fluid into his mouth when he'd gone off to the men's room. Back at our table, he'd blown this out in a spray over a cigarette lighter. This was done, I suppose, to make the conversation more scintillating. And he did have his reputation to uphold.

Combining elements of my father's training with Dr. Thompson's less flamboyant tip, I've come up with an exercise for creative writing students.

▪▪▪ THE EXERCISE ▪▪▪▪▪▪▪▪▪▪▪▪▪▪▪▪▪▪▪▪▪▪▪▪▪▪▪▪▪▪

1. Select a page from a story you're working on. Now rewrite this page in a radically different style. For instance, if your style is basically minimalist, rewrite your page in the style of Melville, Trollope, or Henry James. Or if your sentences are well upholstered, rewrite with Shaker simplicity.

2. Read your original page aloud to the class. Then read the stylistic "translation." Don't be discouraged by smiles from the class. Almost inevitably, something mildly amusing will emerge.

3. Analyze the difference between your original work and the translation.

   a. How is the syntax altered? Cleanth Brooks and Robert Penn Warren suggest that Hemingway's compound sentences, with their simple conjunction *(and)*, reflect a certain philosophy of life. A radically different philosophy might be conveyed by more convoluted syntax. Can you see any reason for this connection between syntax and philosophy?

b. How is the diction altered?

c. Do you have a new feel for the rhythm of your own sentences after doing this translation?

d. Do you find more repetition of words and phrases in your translation? If so, what might account for this?

e. Has the content itself been subtly altered in any way? Do the diction and syntax of another century provide unintended overtones?

f. Exactly why do some moments in your translation seem amusing? Look closely at the metaphors and similes. What about the idiomatic phrases? For example, in James's "The Middle Years," we are told that the "Countess had picked him [a young doctor] up at an hotel..." Characters in Trollope frequently "make love" in public, as well. And a bishop might "ejaculate" a mild oath. Do you think readers of the future might find some of our own expressions quaint and amusing? How intelligible is your diction to older readers? Should this be of any concern at all?

SUGGESTED READING

The Paradise of Bachelors and *The Tartarus of Maids* by Herman Melville.

The Warden by Anthony Trollope.

"On Criticism" by C.S. Lewis, in *Of Other Worlds: Essays and Stories.*

Advice

This exercise should help you see how intimately wedded diction, syntax, and content are in fiction. Too often we take for granted that our own voice is somehow totally natural, perhaps because we write sincerely. But when you take a step back, you hear things differently. For instance, hearing your own voice for the first time on a recording might give you a shock of non-recognition. *That can't be me!* Seeing our own writing from another perspective will help us harmonize the different strains of our complex lineage.

PLOT BUSTER

Aimee Bender

This is an exercise I've done to demonstrate fairy tale plot development—how, in a fairy tale, the story moves along, and fast. It can be really a treat to let go of motivation and just let things happen—let the action reveal the psychology of the character, even let the landscape do that work. It's an exercise in cutting out the internal information (*she thought, she wondered, she realized*) and allowing it to evolve from the storytelling itself.

▪▪▪ THE EXERCISE ▪▪▪▪▪▪▪▪▪▪▪▪▪▪▪▪▪▪▪▪▪▪▪▪▪▪▪▪▪▪▪▪

You need index cards or scraps of paper.

On one scrap of paper, write down an occupation. Or a type of person. It can be a grandmother, or a troll, or a doctor, or a business tycoon.

Hold onto the paper.

On the second piece of paper, write down a verb of any kind. Some sort of action word.

Pass the occupation slip to the person on your right, the verb slip to the person on your left. (If you are doing this exercise alone rather than in a class, I recommend writing a whole slew of occupations and verbs, perhaps even gathering them from books and various papers lying around, and then picking from the pile, to preserve a certain randomness; it's most effective if you don't plan the combination.)

Then, use a fairy tale opener as the starting line. Either:

Once there was a _____ , *who could* _____ .

Or

Once there was a _____ , *who could not* _____ .

Or something along those lines.

Oddly, even with people/verbs that have nothing, supposedly, in common, something often ends up ringing true in the combo.

Then, write forward, without thought, just seeing how the brain makes the logical leap from one word to the next.

SUGGESTED READING

William Maxwell's *The Old Man at the Railroad Crossing;* Italo Calvino's essay "Quickness" in *Six Memos for the Next Millennium;* Isak Dinesen's, "The Blue Jar" as a short-short that moves very fast, through many years, and still has tons of depth and resonance.

Advice

Have fun with it. Plow on ahead; try not to think or plan. Surprise yourself. You can edit and rethink it later; I'd even recommend setting a timer for 15 minutes and just going, forcing yourself to go ahead for the time allotted, even if you get stuck. When stuck, characters can also be stuck—that's the nice thing about writing! If you do this every day for a week, by the end of the week, it's likely that you'll have something interesting to work with.

UNSUNG JOYS OF THE MICRO-EDIT

Steven Heighton

In this era of word processing, it has become common for writers to edit in a skimming sort of way. We've all done this—we've all surfed our eyes over lines of text as they flicker on the screen of our laptops or personal computers. It's a mistake, of course. Editing well demands a word-by-word engagement with the text, not a rough read through, sentence by sentence or paragraph by paragraph. This is not to say that a rapid, skimming read—to get a sense of the general shape, structure, or overall narrative trajectory of a story—doesn't have a place in the larger editorial process. It does, to be sure. That's the macro-edit. But—to keep in the spirit of *writing as re-enaction* (see page 42)—I want to propose a second exercise that attends to the microscopic groundwork, the very foundation of a text: the words on the page.

Getting the groundwork as right as possible involves, instead of breezy skimming, a tough-minded interrogation of every word, and all the punctuation as well. To some writers, this assertion will sound flatly obvious; to others, punitive and masochistic. Most new writers will be in the latter camp. Not that the temptation to skim is restricted to newer writers—every writer feels it to some degree, especially in this accelerated culture. But the disinclined reviser can learn to enjoy the feeling of sharpening and tightening the prose (or, if necessary, fleshing it out) till every word feels integral, nailed to the page, permanent. Excess and imprecision create a sort of blurring effect not unlike the television static caused by bad reception; locating and cutting what's unneeded brings the "picture" into sharp focus, allowing things to leap to clarity.

▪▪▪ THE EXERCISE ▪▪▪▪▪▪▪▪▪▪▪▪▪▪▪▪▪▪▪▪▪▪▪▪▪▪▪▪▪

In a workshop seminar, the exercise goes like this: using a paragraph from a Mavis Gallant story (though any good story or novel would do), the participants and I edit a piece of formerly excellent prose. The prose is no longer excellent because I have retro-edited it—i.e., padded it with unnecessary connectives and redundant adverbs; muddied it with imprecise, hackneyed, or superfluous adjectives; de-intensified it by replacing the original verbs with less exact ones; land-mined it with colloquial clichés; and otherwise defaced and polluted it. It's important that I not take this fun project of editorial vandalism too far. The paragraph must still read with plausible fluency. It should make sense. It should look okay on quick inspection. At any rate, I write this retro-edited version on a blackboard or whiteboard, to allow for quick erasures and insertions, then reveal what I've done and ask the students to scrutinize the paragraph word by word.

I've found that it's rarely necessary to kick things off by saying, for example, "I wonder if we need this word here?" The natural zeal for criticizing other people's work, especially in their absence, will briskly emerge and students will start pointing out things that can be improved, or cut. Like that idle second or third adjective you've added to the original one or two ("an idle, loitering, inactive adjective"). Like the adverb modifying a verb that already implies its meaning ("she strides quickly across the plaza"; "he berates her vehemently"). Like the flabby filler words that are a natural part of speech or of any written first draft but which are now clotting up the prose ("he didn't really think anything about it in particular, but, all the same, it was always there in his mind").

In my experience, once students get involved in this exercise there's no stopping them. Almost everyone weighs in. Arguments break out. And, inevitably, several students will suggest improvements where I've made no changes at all—and by having to explain their suggestions, then defend them (when I tell them they're now editing Gallant's original prose), they gain confidence, as well as a sense that rewriting in this way can be, if not quite pleasurable, then exciting, a challenge, a test of one's discipline and powers of perception. The aim is to incite an enthusiasm for micro-editing that the participants will then apply to their own work. Because, as we all know and as we see every time a group workshops a story, it's much easier to spot the flaws in someone else's writing. I suggest writers sit down with a printout of their own first or second or third drafts and imagine that I've secretly tampered with their prose in the same way I did with Gallant's. And now work it back toward its "original," and final, form.

Here are the first few sentences—in their corrupted and then in their pristine form—of the Gallant paragraph I usually use when I do this exercise with a group. It's from one of her best-known stories, "An Autobiography." As you'll see, Gallant's prose suits the purpose of this exercise perfectly because it's so spare and austere:

> I can recall, in calm, windless, spring woods, my eyes fixed on the ground, searching it for poisonous mushrooms. He would sharply knock them out of the soft, squelchy ground with his briarwood walking stick, and I would conscientiously tread them to pulp. I now teach my pupils to do the very same thing ... etc.

> I recall, in calm woods, my eyes on the ground, searching for poisonous mushrooms. He knocked them out of the soft ground with his walking stick, and I conscientiously trod them to pulp. I teach my pupils to do the same ... etc.

SUGGESTED READING

Reading great prose, a few lines at a time, with careful attention to the arrangement of the words, would of course be a good complement to this exercise.

Advice

Stand on the side of artifice—of worked and earned, elaborated form. Life gives us enough of life. We approach art for something different—more distilled, catalyzed, charged, and signifying.

THE WORLD'S WORST SHORT STORY CONTEST

A. Manette Ansay

We spend a lot of time in writing classes talking about what makes a well-written story: an engaging narrative voice; round and original characters; a compelling plot that, in the end, is both surprising and inevitable. This exercise is designed to emphasize good writing by focusing, without warning, on its opposite.

▪▪▪ THE EXERCISE ▪▪▪▪▪▪▪▪▪▪▪▪▪▪▪▪▪▪▪▪▪▪▪▪▪▪▪▪▪▪▪▪▪▪▪

Have the students divide themselves into groups of three and four. I announce that they have the next forty minutes or so to write the World's Worst Short Story, by which I mean the most clichéd, hackneyed, technically absurd, *cheesiest* story anybody has ever put to paper. I'll tell them that they'll be competing for a prize. (In the past, my prizes have included a torn-bodice novel and an incredibly tacky pen, but recently I've discovered that a super-sized bag of Nacho Cheese Doritos with *They're the cheesiest!* scrawled across the front generates the most excitement.)

When the more literal-minded of the students ask questions—"Do you mean we should write with bad grammar?"—use this as an opportunity to do a sneaky review of some of the things I've been teaching them to avoid: inappropriate Latinate diction (*I partook of my lunch in the cafeteria*), strained dialogue tags (*"Oh, yes!" he ejaculated*), unnecessary adverbs (*"Stop!" Jane yelled loudly*), and conceptual repetition (*"Stop!" Jane yelled loudly, and at the top of her lungs, with great energy*). I get them laughing over these (and other) examples. I point out that the result of each of these pitfalls is, inevitably, the use of clichéd language. Clichéd language builds stock characters. Stock characters create familiar situations. I rattle the bag of Doritos and tell them that this is exactly the kind of thinking I'm looking for. By now, the students should be realizing that writing really *good* bad fiction is going to require some serious thought.

On your mark, get set, go.

SUGGESTED READING

We probably see enough of this bad fiction without having to seek it out. However, if you're a glutton for punishment, there are a host of bad-writing contests out there, including the Bulwer-Lytton Fiction Contest (Edward George Bulwer-Lytton wrote the interminable opening line beginning, *It was a dark and stormy night* ...); the International Imitation Hemingway Contest; and the Faux Faulkner Contest, all of which have online sites you can find through any search engine.

Advice

This exercise is a great mid-semester or mid-conference energizer, because it allows the students to get a little silly while, at the same time, reviewing what they've learned. It doesn't work at the beginning of the semester, when students are at wildly different levels of critical sophistication and someone could bring everything to a halt by defending, for example, the use of clichés.

DECONSTRUCTING BEDS

Alison Fell

This is an excellent exercise for anyone suffering from blocks or general stodginess in their prose or poetry writing. It encourages writers to relax their control of language in order to allow a lighter and fuller control to emerge. This exercise can be done over two sessions or classes.

▪▪▪ THE EXERCISE ▪▪▪▪▪▪▪▪▪▪▪▪▪▪▪▪▪▪▪▪▪▪▪▪▪▪▪▪▪▪▪▪▪

1. Ask participants to write a hundred words of prose describing a bed they slept in as a child. It needn't be perfect Virginia Woolf–style prose—it's only raw material, but they should write in sentences rather than in note form, as the verbs will become important later.

2. Next, have them write another hundred words on the bed they currently occupy—what's in it, what surrounds it, what they do in it, etc. We spend one-third of our lives in bed, but no one seems to write about it!

3. Have them write a final hundred words on a fantasy bed, a bed where money is no object, a bed that can be made of

anything they like. (When I was working out this exercise initially, I found myself inventing a bed made of meringue and chocolate.) This step may prove more difficult than the previous two; participants should feel free to let themselves go to town on it.

4. It's interesting to read back over the three descriptions at this stage, because of the common strands that may be emerging in the past, present, and fantasy beds. This preliminary stage of the exercise can also be useful for characterization in a novel or story: to imagine what sort of bed your fictional character slept/sleeps/would like to sleep in brings you in quite close, I think, and is a tactic I've used myself when in difficulty.

5. For the second stage of the exercise, which I usually do in the following week's session, ask participants to bring with them their three hundred words, typed up and cut into very short phrases and single words, tucked into an envelope. It's as well to have scissors and glue around, as I've found that some participants will cling to favorite or fancy phrases and have to be encouraged to dismember them. Of course, others will have left predictable or clichéd phrases intact. For instance, I always ask people to separate *book* from *shelves,* and *chest* from *drawers,* leaving the way open for, say, *a chest of tortoises.* I also ask them to fracture the subject of a sentence from the object, the noun from its verb, etc., so that as many elements as possible may be set free to play their part—and *play* is the operative word—in a completely new composition.

6. Now have participants lay out all their words and short phrases so that they can be scanned easily by eye. Then ask participants to assemble short sequences, intuitively, without

worrying about commonsensical things like meaning or narrative. At this point, the rationalists, bless them, will object that the results of such a process can only be random nonsense, which one can counter by pointing out that this would be true only if the words were assembled while face down! I think it's important to make the point that words don't need to be whipped into line all the time by some big boss writer (in fact, they hate it, and will probably dig their heels in and refuse to be of any service). Given a little space, they will play together creatively. Given a little love, they will love you back.

One thing I do stress at this point is to use conventional syntax as much as possible in the reassemblage—for syntax provides a holding frame for the new, nonrealist images and meanings. Otherwise participants should be encouraged to keep an open mind and allow their themes to emerge, rather than try to reproduce their original pieces in any way. It's important that the unconscious be given permission to play its part—which indeed it does, judging by the reactions of surprise, recognition, even illumination, when the writer sees what new motifs are emerging.

This work takes a long time—at least two hours or so. The new short sequences should be put to one side or written down. Later they can be rearranged, verb tenses unified if you want, and so on. I encourage people to use as many of their words as possible, especially if it's their first encounter with collage. When they are more confident, they will scan more fluently, very quickly take what they need from the selection of words in front of them, and discard the rest.

Finally, have participants read out their finished pieces. These
will be very open texts which, compared to naturalistic prose,
make big demands on the listener. (However, it's always good
for students to be aware that the reader is willing to *work*. How
hard is another question, of course.) I ask everyone to make
notes during the readings, to see if there is any consensus about
which images and sequences resonate, and why they do. Also, of
course, to provide a response for the writer who's reading out.
Some of the fascinating elements that have emerged from these
discussions are the way abstract or concept words—e.g., *health,
jealousy,* or *dissatisfaction*—can engage with concrete words—
e.g., anything you can perceive with the five senses, like *fence-
post, lightning,* or *growl.* When allowed to happen, these
abstract-concrete alliances can challenge the distinction between
"inner" and "outer" spaces and articulate poetic truths. Then
there is also the joy of surreal juxtapositions and distortions, the
determination of words to combine along the lines of sound
systems—assonance, consonance, etc.—and last, but not least at
all, there's the certainty of encountering at least one or two
images of breathtaking originality!

In the end, even the fact that the texts contain things that can't
be pinned down exactly, and raise questions that can't always be
answered, seems to me to be important in these days of debased
mediaspeak and empty, formulaic language. It's no bad thing for
writers to pay a little homage to the indefinable once in a while,
to "learn to love the questions themselves," as Rilke so wisely
advised.

DETAILS (GOLDEN), CHARACTER (IMMORTAL) AND SETTING (RURAL INDIA)

Dave Eggers

My classes are two hours long, and for this first session, I'm trying to do the following things:

- Get the students thinking about specificity in their writing

- Get them thinking about the value of personal observation

- Get them better acquainted with each other

- Get them started on a short story that challenges them to solve fairly sophisticated problems of setting and motive

■■■ THE EXERCISE ■■■■■■■■■■■■■■■■■■■■■■■■■■■■■■■■■■■■■■

Step One: The Power of Observation *(12 minutes)*

Start with the head of a stuffed crocodile. Or something like that. 826 Valencia is next to a store that sells taxidermied animals, so I usually go over and borrow one of their crocodile heads. Whatever you choose to use, this object should be something fairly unusual, but it should also be something that the students have seen before. Now—without showing the students the object—pass out blank pieces of paper, and ask the students to draw the object. For example, if I have the stuffed crocodile head hidden in my desk, I will tell the students, "You have five minutes to draw a perfectly accurate rendering of a Peruvian caiman (a type of small crocodile)." The students will laugh, but you will be serious. They have to get down to business, and draw that crocodile.

After five minutes, most students will have a pretty sorry-looking crocodile. They will have drawn the animal from memory, trying to recall if the crocodile's eyes are on the top of its head, or the side, and if the teeth are inside its mouth or protrude out the sides. Collect the drawings and show them to the class. Guffaws will follow.

Now take the actual crocodile head out, and place it somewhere where all the students can easily see it. Now ask them to draw the Peruvian caiman again, using the actual animal as a model. After five minutes, you'll see a tremendous difference. Where there was guessing and vagueness and error in the first drawings, there will be detail, specificity, and accuracy now that the students can refer to the genuine article. They'll see that the eyes are actually on top of its head. They'll see that the eyes are like a cat's—eerie and many-layered. They'll see that the snout is very long, very narrow, and very brittle-seeming.

Step Two: Apply the Lesson of the Peruvian Caiman to Any and All Writing *(5 minutes)*

The lesson is pretty clear. If you draw from life, from observation, your writing will be more convincing. It doesn't matter if you're writing science fiction, fantasy, or contemporary realism—whatever it is, it will benefit from real-life observation. Is there a street performer in the novel you're writing? Go watch one in action. Is there a short-haired terrier in the story you're writing? Go observe one. Is there a meat-eating Venus flytrap plant in your poem? See how they really do it. Nothing can substitute for the level of specificity you get when you actually observe.

Step Three: Knowing the Difference in Details
(25 minutes)

My students and I talk about the three types of details. With different classes, we've given these three types different names, but here we'll call them:

Golden

Useful

Not-so-good

Now let's try to define them, in reverse order so we have some drama:

Not-so-good: This is a very nice way of referring to clichés or clunky descriptions or analogies. First, clichés: If there's one service we can give to these students, it's to wean them off the use of clichés. Clichés just destroy everything in their path, and they prevent the student's writing from being personal or original. *He was as strong as an ox. She ate like a bird. His hands were clammy. She looked like she'd seen a ghost.* There's just no point, really, in writing these words down. When students can tell a cliché when they see one, they become better critical thinkers, better readers, smarter people. When they learn to stay away from clichés in their own writing, they're on their way to becoming far stronger writers. The other type of not-so-good detail is a clunky one. *His* *legs looked like square-cut carrots. Her dog was like a blancmange crossed with high-plains cowboy.* This is, in a way, preferable to a cliché, but it's so strange and hard to picture that it disrupts the flow of the story.

Useful: These are descriptions that are plain but needed. *His hair was orange. Her face was long and oval.* These pedestrian details are necessary, of course. Not every description can be golden. Speaking of which:

Golden: This is a detail/description/analogy that's singular, completely original, and makes one's subject unforgettable. *She tapped her fingernail rhythmically on her large teeth as she watched her husband count the change in his man-purse.* In one sentence, we've learned so much about these two people. He has a man-purse. He's fastidious. She's tired of him. She's exasperated by him. She has large teeth. Golden details can come about even while using plain words: *Their young daughter's eyes were grey and cold, exhausted.* These words, individually bland, are very specific and unsettling when applied to a young girl. In one key sentence, a writer can nail down a character. This is a sample from one of my students, describing a man she saw in the park near 826 Valencia: *He wore a beret, though he'd never been to Paris, and he walked like a dancer, as if hoping someone would notice that he walked like a dancer.*

Working this out with the class: Getting the students understanding the differences between these three kinds of description is possible with an exercise that's always good fun. Create a chart, where you have three categories: Not-so-good; Useful; Golden. Now give them a challenge: come up with examples of each. Tell them that they need to conjure examples for, say:

The feeling of traveling at 100 miles per hour.

The students in one of my classes came up with these:

Not-so-good: like flying; like being on a rollercoaster; so fast you want to puke; like being shot out of a canon

Useful: terrifying; dizzying; nerve-racking; hurtling

Golden: like being dropped down a well; as the speed grew, I heard death's whisper grow louder and louder

The exploration of these types of description can last a full class period, for sure. If you want to keep going, consider this one game I use sometimes. This takes the concept to a new level of fun.

Step Four: Interviewing Your Peers While Observing Them Shrewdly *(15 minutes)*

Start by telling the students that they're going to interview each other for fifteen minutes. The students will be paired up—try to pair up students who don't usually talk to each other much—and they'll find a quiet place to talk. One will interview the other, and after seven and a half minutes, they'll switch. Before getting them started, talk about what sorts of details are useful in defining a character, making that character singular and intriguing. They'll be applying what they know from the caiman exercise, and also using good interviewing techniques, to immediately get beyond the "Where do you go to school" sorts of questions. By asking good questions and observing closely, the interviews should produce strong results very quickly, now that the students know that they're looking for golden details.

Step Five: Immortalizing Your Subject *(30 minutes)*

Once all the students have notes about their assigned peers, you can do one of two things:

The Simple but Essential Character Sketch

You can ask them to simply write one-page character sketches of their peers, which should be compelling, true, well-observed, and (of course) beautifully written. This alone is a very worthwhile assignment. When these are read aloud, the interview subjects benefit from what in most cases is the first time they've ever been thus defined. It's strange but true: it's pretty rare to have someone observe you closely, write about your gestures and freckles and manner of speech. In the process, the interviewers improve their powers of observation, while the interviewees blush and can't get the words out of their brain. And the pairs of students get to know each other far better than they would almost any other way. It's a good way to break through cliques, create new bonds of understanding.

Place Your Subject in Rural India (for example)

The lesson works pretty well either way, but something extraordinary happens with this second part, the curveball part. At this stage, after the first 15 minutes, hand out pictures to the students. These pictures, one per student, should depict some unusual, strange, foreign, bizarre, or historical setting. Usually I make copies from old LIFE books about the various cultures of the world. Thus some student might end up with a picture of a Swedish farm, a royal Thai court, a Nairobi marketplace, or a scene from rural India. Then tell the class that they need to (a) use the details they've gathered about their classmate; and then (b) place that student in this foreign setting. The writers then need to concoct a reason that their character is in rural India or in Barbados, Grenada, or the drawing room of a Scottish duke. This requires the writer to imagine this new/strange world and also to solve the problem of what the character is doing there. Is she stuck; is she trying to leave? How would this student react to being lost in a marketplace in Nairobi? Who or what is he looking for?

If you have some time, or want to expand the exercise, have the students research their location a bit. Even by using the picture alone, they are using their observational powers, but with the added benefit of some book-oriented or internet research, they can conjure ever-more convincing settings.

I have to admit that I came up with this exercise on the fly. I had no idea that it would work, but it did the first time I did it, and it always works. Here's why:

- The process of interviewing their classmates is always appealing to students.

- The close observation makes both students—interviewer and interviewee—feel valued and singular.

- The curveball of putting the interviewee in a foreign setting forces this student outside his or her own school/home/neighborhood and requires the solving of a fairly sophisticated problem: Who is this person and why is he or she here? The drama and conflict are built into the setting, and they get a short story off to a quick and intriguing start.

MORE WRITER'S GYM EXERCISES

PLACES, PLEASE

Creating a story with a good sense of exactly where it's taking place is very important. It's what makes readers remember your story. We anchor ourselves in the world based on *where:* where we live; where we work, eat, fall in love; where we go for enter-tainment, worship, etc. A character without a location is floating a little too freely, and that will limit your story quite profoundly. Even if you're writing about Anytown, USA, you must create a world for your fictional people to inhabit.

▪▪▪ THE EXERCISE ▪▪▪▪▪▪▪▪▪▪▪▪▪▪▪▪▪▪▪▪▪▪▪▪▪▪▪▪▪▪▪▪▪▪▪▪

Think of a location you pass every day or often, or someplace you have been *very* curious about in the city/town/hamlet where you live. Examples: a strange house you walk by en route to work, an old shop that's never actually open for business, a coffee shop that's different from others. Antique shops, tailors, and other individualized businesses can yield possibilities, as can really intimidating structures. Or, you can choose a place that gives you the creeps, someplace you've been that made you feel uneasy, that you visited once and hope never to return to. Then you can explore *why,* using fictional techniques: make up something dramatic.

It really helps to choose a place you've been curious about for a time, because a sense of mystery will lead you to wondering, which is how you find the characters for this particular story. Try not to base the characters too literally on real people you have seen connected to the place, although, by all means, use them for inspiration for inventing the story. You're not just writing a five- to ten-page description of the place itself: you'll need to wonder about the people connected to it, past, present, and future. Who would live/work/eat/etc. there? What would they do in that place? What has happened to make the place what it is today? Think dramatically: if you choose a sandwich shop, it wouldn't be fun or interesting reading if we simply watched someone make sandwiches for ten pages, right?

In the first paragraph, focus exclusively on letting the reader see, smell, feel, hear, and even taste the place you have chosen; then move into the character aspect, introducing us to someone very connected to the location. Let your own curiosity be your guide as you create a plot evolving from the sense of place in the story.

SUGGESTED READING

Toni Morrison's novels *Jazz* and *Paradise* manage to create kingdoms in a way that's memorable. Morrison's ability to create a sense of place is directly connected to her use of the five senses in her work. She never neglects to mention the smell and sound and look of a place, and you can also feel the air in her worlds. Used sparingly, sense-driven detail can put you in the big league of fiction.

Advice

If *you* feel bored writing it and can't quite see the world you're expecting your characters to live in, your reader can't be expected to respond in a deep way. That said, you may think you've done the work of place-making: let a fresh pair of eyes be the judge and ask someone you trust to give you feedback. Also, a writer who doesn't travel whenever possible isn't exercising the powerful faculty of observing new environments and new sensory triggers. You don't need to write about exotic places, but do be mindful of the fact that a true understanding of one's homeland often comes from leaving it for a time.

DOUBLED DRAMA

Good drama comes from the unfolding of a main event and at least one sub-event that unfolds at the same time. The character who wants more than one thing is always a more interesting read. Think in terms of your own levels of want: I want to get through this day, I want a Mercedes because it will make me look rich, I want to find the love of my life—where is he? Think too of movies or TV dramas you love: there is never just one story event happening, but rather, a main one and then one or two sub-stories that enrich the central plot. If anything, the sub-plots increase the dramatic tension as the reader/viewer wonders how the main characters will cope with simultaneous stressors. Comedies also have this form of converging events as the source of much hilarity. Doubled drama only ever increases the stakes for what the main characters want, and that's good: that's layered writing a reader won't soon forget.

■■■ THE EXERCISE ■■■■■■■■■■■■■■■■■■■■■■■■■■■■■■■■■■■■

For this one, you can either expand an existing/rough draft story by adding a subplot, or you can begin a new story that features a main plot plus some secondary storyline that nevertheless enhances the drama of the main plotline somehow. Here are some good examples of secondary storylines: character, already facing potential disaster at work, hears of an impending visitor (much wanted or very unwanted); main character faces a deadline of some kind in personal or professional life on top of current conflict; private personal drama makes it hard for main character to keep other conflict under control.

Facades are also excellent: the double lives of characters have created much drama in fiction, especially when the facades crack. Say the character lives one life by day, another by night; one life today, another by the week's end, etc. Who people are at work versus who they might be at home and the contrast therein—that's interesting character work.

Have fun using a side story to enhance the drama of the main story. This is an important concept in story writing. Consider the psychology, motives, and even the economic positions of various minor characters who might make your main character's situation harder during the story. Sometimes the seemingly minor drama ends up taking over to great effect. The bottom line: the reader asks, What's important in life? and that's what we, as writers, are trying to determine every time we sit down to work.

SUGGESTED READING

In this instance, a movie is in fact the best example of levels of want, and various events and substories unfolding. *Changing Lanes*, starring Ben Affleck and Samuel L. Jackson, is a terrific example of doubled drama: each man has a private life with its own challenges and stakes in addition to the core event. The "minor" dramas of their lives actually drive them to cherish even more potently the event's outcome. That's *doubled drama.*

Advice

Is there only one thing you want in your own life? Not likely. Explore some of your secret wants and dreams and let them flow through characters whenever possible. Think about a typical week in your life and assess the levels of want, the doubled-up events. That's actually the true essence of the old saw "Write what you know." It could be better understood by most of us as "Write what you quietly, ferociously desire."

FOUNDATIONS OF CHARACTER

A writer's whole arsenal of stories and characters stems from a rich, often unconscious well-spring. Very often our fears, desires, and wishes of how things could be generate powerful writing.

■■■ THE EXERCISE ■■■■■■■■■■■■■■■■■■■■■■■■■■■■■■■■■■

Part One

This portion of the exercise is wholly personal in nature. It's about you, and should be done as quickly as possible with as much privacy as possible, and written long-hand at double-size, meaning writ large, literally. The slight discomfort of writing in larger scrawl works magic. Besides, this is just for you, not for sharing. Be as honest as possible, and if you feel like writing long answers to each, feel free. Keep this information someplace private, or invest in a shredder. Once written down, it imprints on your imagination anyway. Many a writer has been thwarted by a partner or friend mortified by the discovery of such lists.

1. Write fifteen statements that are "true" about you, including a mix of physical, emotional, and skills-related traits.

2. List ten things you *wish* were true about you.

3. What is your first conscious memory?

4. What scares you most? (Examples: public speaking, driving, flying in a hot air balloon, visiting a war-torn country.)

5. List five things that enrage you; not just annoyances, but things, people, and events that arouse genuine anger/rage.

6. List two things you wish you'd never seen/encountered.

7. List two things you wish you'd never said, or occasions where you behaved badly that can still make you wince.

8. List eleven things that bring you happiness and pleasure.

Part Two

Read over this list of things about you. Using some of the answers from this self-driven questionnaire, create a piece of fiction of at least ten pages in length. The story must have some form of plot.

In order to "fictionalize," we take what is true or reality based and bend it somehow, both for our own psychic privacy as well as for dramatic effect: sometimes the whole truth is a bit dull (not always, but sometimes) and we need to exaggerate the circumstances or actions. Names and locations change and shift, but the deeper essence comes directly from the writer.

SUGGESTED READING

Read some F. Scott Fitzgerald novels and stories and then read *Zelda,* the biography of Zelda Fitzgerald by Nancy Milford, to see just how this subliminal process works. It isn't about an accurate depiction of what went on, but rather, how emotions and events filter down into fictional works.

Advice

Get to know someone other than yourself/your partner. Talk to strangers, leave the house and have a life. Writers who only write will eventually dry up. A writer is someone who has a passion for studying human nature—a scholarship best done on the front lines. Ask questions, daily, especially of complete strangers. You'll be amazed by the candid answers you receive—and you'll never lack for material.

ABOUT THE CONTRIBUTORS

Steve Almond is the author of two story collections, *My Life in Heavy Metal* and *The Evil B.B. Chow,* the nonfiction book *Candyfreak,* and the novel (with Julianna Baggott) *Which Brings Me to You*. His next book will be a collection of essays, to be published in 2007.

Gail Anderson-Dargatz's novels have been published worldwide in English and in many other languages. *A Recipe for Bees* and *The Cure for Death by Lightning* were international bestsellers, and were both short-listed for the prestigious Giller Prize in Canada. *The Cure for Death by Lightning* won the UK's Betty Trask Prize among other awards. *A Rhinestone Button* was a national bestseller in Canada, and her first book, *The Miss Hereford Stories*, was short-listed for the Stephen Leacock Medal. She currently teaches fiction in the creative writing MFA program at the University of British Columbia and lives in the Shuswap, the landscape found in so much of her writing including her upcoming novel, *Turtle Valley*.

A. Manette Ansay's first novel, *Vinegar Hill,* was published in 1994, followed by a story collection, *Read This and Tell Me What It Says,* in 1995. She has since published three more novels: *Sister* (1996), *River Angel* (1998), and *Midnight Champagne* (1999), which was a finalist for the National Book Critics Circle Award. *Vinegar Hill* was chosen by Oprah Winfrey as her November 1999 Book Club selection. Ansay's memoir, *Limbo,* was published in 2001. Currently she teaches in the MFA program at the University of Miami in Coral Gables, where she is Associate Professor of English. Her latest novel, *Blue Water,* was published in 2006.

Margaret Atwood is the author of more than thirty-five volumes of poetry, fiction, and nonfiction and is perhaps best known for her novels, which include *The Edible Woman* (1970), *The Handmaid's Tale* (1983), *The Robber Bride* (1994), and *Alias Grace* (1996). *The Blind Assassin* won the 2000 Booker Prize, and, in April 2003, her eleventh novel, the Man Booker Prize–nominated *Oryx and Crake* was released to great acclaim. Ms. Atwood's *The Penelopiad,* a retelling of *The Odyssey* from the perspective of Penelope and her maids, was released in the fall of 2005 as part of *The Myths Series* and a collection of mini-fictions, *The Tent,* was published in the winter of 2006. Her most recent publication is a collection of short stories, *Moral Disorder.*

Aimee Bender is the author of three books: *The Girl in the Flammable Skirt, An Invisible Sign of My Own,* and *Willful Creatures.* Her short fiction has been published in *GQ, Granta, The Paris Review, Tin House,* and many more journals and anthologies. She teaches creative writing at the University of Southern California; and before that, she taught elementary school and adult night school, making the age range of her students from four to seventy-four.

T.C. Boyle is the author of nineteen books of fiction, most recently the collection *Tooth and Claw* and the novel *Talk Talk.*

Catherine Bush is the author of three critically acclaimed novels: *Claire's Head* (2004), short-listed for the Trillium Book Award; *The Rules of Engagement* (2000), a *New York Times* Notable Book; and *Minus Time* (1993), short-listed for the Books in Canada First Novel Award. She has taught creative writing at Concordia University, the

University of British Columbia, the University of Florida, and elsewhere, and has also been writer-in-residence at several Canadian universities. Her nonfiction has appeared in numerous publications, including the *New York Times Magazine* and *The Globe and Mail*. She lives in Toronto.

Ron Carlson teaches writing at the University of California at Irvine. His selected stories is *A Kind of Flying* and his novel *Five Skies* is to be published in 2007.

Douglas Coupland is a writer and visual artist who lives and works in Vancouver, British Columbia.

Dave Eggers is the founder of the writing center 826 Valencia and the literary quarterly *McSweeney's.* He is the author of *A Heartbreaking Work of Staggering Genius, You Shall Know Our Velocity!* and *How We Are Hungry,* and coauthor of *Teachers Have It Easy: The Big Sacrifices and Small Salaries of America's Teachers*.

Alison Fell is a Scottish novelist and poet based in London. She has published seven novels, including the prize-winning *Mer de Glace, The Pillow Boy of the Lady Onogoro,* and *Tricks of the Light*; four poetry collections, and three anthologies of experimental women's writing. She has taught creative writing for many years, and has been a Writing Fellow at New South Wales Institute of Technology in Sydney, Australia; University College London; and at the University of East Anglia. She is currently an AHRC Research Fellow in Creative Arts at Middlesex University, London.

Lee Gowan grew up on a farm near Swift Current, Saskatchewan. He is the author of the story collection *Going to Cuba* and the novels *Make Believe Love,* which was nominated for a Trillium Book Award, and *The Last Cowboy*. He currently directs the creative writing program at the School of Continuing Studies, University of Toronto.

Steven Hayward was born and raised in Toronto. His short fiction has won awards at the University of Toronto, the University of North Carolina, and the University of Arkansas. His first book, *Buddha Stevens and Other Stories,* won the 2001 Upper Canada Writers' Craft Award and was a *Globe and Mail* top 100 book of 2001. His novel *The Secret Mitzvah of Lucio Burke* won Italy's Premio Grinzane Cavour prize. Currently he lives in Cleveland Heights, Ohio, with his wife and three children and is a professor of English at John Carroll University.

Steven Heighton is the author of the novel *Afterlands,* which came out in 2005 in Canada and has recently appeared in the United States, where it was a *New York Times Book Review* Editors' Choice. Editions will appear soon in Britain, Australia, Germany, and the Netherlands. He has also published *The Shadow Boxer,* which was a Canadian bestseller and a Publishers Weekly Book of the Year for 2002. His other fiction books are the story collections *Flight Paths of the Emperor* and *On Earth as It Is,* while his poetry collections include *The Ecstasy of Skeptics* and *The Address Book*. His work is translated into nine languages, has been internationally anthologized, and has been nominated for the Governor General's Award, the Trillium Book Award, a Pushcart Prize, the Journey Prize, and Britain's W.H.Smith Award. He has also won the Gerald Lampert Memorial Award, the Petra Kenney Prize, the Air Canada Award, and gold medals for fiction and for poetry in the National Magazine Awards. In 2002–03, he was the writer-in-residence at Concordia University; in 2004 he was the University of Toronto (Massey College) writer-in-residence. He lives with his family in Kingston, Ontario.

Greg Hollingshead has published three story collections and three novels. His collection *The Roaring Girl* (1995) won the Governor General's Award for Fiction. His novel *The Healer* (1998) won the

Rogers Writers' Trust Fiction Prize and was short-listed for the Giller Prize. His latest novel is *Bedlam* (2004). Greg lives in Edmonton, where he is professor emeritus at the University of Alberta. He is also director of writing programs at the Banff Centre.

Richard House is the author of *Bruiser, Uninvited,* and *The Kills*. His fiction has appeared in *Whitewalls, BOMB, discontents,* and the *Village Voice Literary Supplement.*

Frances Itani has written ten books, including the international best-seller *Deafening,* which won a Commonwealth Award for Best Book and was short-listed for the 2005 IMPAC Dublin Literary Award and William Saroyan International Prize for Writing. Other books include the prize-winning *Poached Egg on Toast* and *Leaning, Leaning over Water*. She taught creative writing for many years and lives in Ottawa, where she is working on a novel, *Celebration*.

W. Todd Kaneko currently lives and writes in Tempe, Arizona. He has an MFA in Creative Writing from Arizona State University, and his work has appeared recently in *Roanoke Review*.

Toby Litt was born in 1968. His most recent novel is *Ghost Story*. He co-edited *New Writing 13* with Ali Smith. He is a Granta Best of Young British Novelist. His website is at www.tobylitt.com.

Margot Livesey was born and grew up on the edge of the Scottish Highlands. After taking a BA in literature and philosophy at the University of York in England, she spent most of her twenties in Toronto writing and waitressing. Subsequently she moved to America, where she has taught in a number of colleges and universities, including Massachusetts's Williams College, the Warren Wilson MFA Program, and the Iowa Writers' Workshop. She has received grants from the National Endowment for the Arts and the Guggenheim Foundation and is the author of a collection of stories and five novels, including *Criminals, Eva Moves the Furniture,* and, most recently, *Banishing Verona*. She now lives mostly in Boston and is currently a writer-in-residence at Emerson College in Boston.

Val McDermid is the author of twenty-three books, including *Wire in the Blood* (adapted into a popular TV series in Britain), *The Torment of Others, The Distant Echo, The Grave Tattoo,* and *A Place of Execution*.

Rick Moody's first novel, *Garden State,* was the winner of the 1991 Editor's Choice Award from the Pushcart Press. *The Ice Storm* (1994) has been published in twenty countries and a film version directed by Ang Lee was released by Fox Searchlight in 1997. His other internationally acclaimed novels and story collections are *Purple America, Demonology, The Ring of Brightest Angels, The Black Veil: A Memoir with Digressions,* and *The Diviners*. His fiction and journalism has been anthologized in *Best American Short Stories 2001, Best American Essays 2004*, and the *Pushcart Prize Anthology* among others. Rick Moody has taught at the State University of New York at Purchase, the Bennington College Writing Seminars, the Fine Arts Work Center in Provincetown, and the New School for Social Research in New York City. He lives in Brooklyn, New York.

Alix Ohlin is the author of the novel *The Missing Person* (2005) and the short story collection *Babylon and Other Stories* (2006). She teaches at Lafayette College in Easton, Pennsylvania.

Kate Pullinger's most recent novel is *A Little Stranger*. Other books include the novels *Weird Sister, The Last Time I Saw Jane,* and *Where Does Kissing End?* and the short story collections *My Life as a Girl in a Men's Prison* and *Tiny Lies*. Kate Pullinger writes for film, radio, and new media; her multimedia online novel, *Inanimate Alice* (www.inanimatealice.com), created with web artist babel, won the first prize for Digital Art 2005, sponsored by MAXXI (the Museum of the Twenty-First Century, in Rome) and Fondazione Rosselli. She is Reader in Creative Writing and New Media at De Montfort University, Leicester, UK. Kate Pullinger grew up in Canada and now lives in London, England. Her website is at www.katepullinger.com.

Andrew Pyper is the author of three bestselling novels, most recently *The Wildfire Season* (2005), *The Trade Mission* (2002), and *Lost Girls* (1999), as well as *Kiss Me* (1996), a collection of short stories. He lives in Toronto.

Michael Redhill is a novelist, playwright, and poet. His most recent works are *Goodness*, a play, and *Consolation*, a novel. He lives and works in Toronto.

Elizabeth Ruth's debut novel, *Ten Good Seconds of Silence,* was published in 2001 and named a finalist for the Rogers' Writers' Trust Fiction Prize, the Amazon.ca/Books in Canada First Novel Award, and the Toronto Book Award. Elizabeth's second novel, *Smoke,* was published to critical acclaim in 2005. *The Globe and Mail* called *Smoke* "a virtuoso performance." Both novels have sold internationally. She also publishes short fiction and nonfiction for journals, magazines, and newspapers across the country. Elizabeth Ruth has taught creative writing for many years, and currently does so through the school of Continuing Studies at the University of Toronto. She will also be teaching in the correspondence program at the Humber School for Writers in 2007. Her website is at www.elizabethruth.com.

Antanas Sileika's most recent novel, *Woman in Bronze,* was listed as a *Globe and Mail* Best Book of 2004. Antanas Sileika is the Artistic Director of the Humber School for Writers.

Priscila Uppal is a poet and fiction writer born in Ottawa and currently living in Toronto. Among her publications are five collections of poetry—*How to Draw Blood from a Stone* (1998), *Confessions of a Fertility Expert* (1999), *Pretending to Die* (2001), *Live Coverage* (2003), and *Ontological Necessities* (2006)—and the novel *The Divine Economy of Salvation* (2002), published to critical acclaim in Canada and the United States and translated into Dutch and Greek. Her poetry has been translated into Korean, Croatian, Latvian, and Italian. She has a PhD in English literature and is a professor of Humanities at Toronto's York University and Coordinator of the Creative Writing Program.

Elizabeth Weld recently graduated from the MFA program at Arizona State University. Her work has appeared in *Arts & Letters, Crazyhorse, Shenandoah,* and *The Gettysburg Review*. She lives in Tempe, Arizona.

James Wilcox's stories have appeared in *The New Yorker, Avenue,* and *Louisiana Literature.* His eight novels include *Modern Baptists* and *Heavenly Days*. A graduate of Yale University, he was a recipient of a Guggenheim Fellowship. Currently, he is Director of Creative Writing at Louisiana State University in Baton Rouge.

Marnie Woodrow is the author of two short story collections and a novel, *Spelling Mississippi*. A recipient of the Excellence in Teaching Award at the University of Toronto School of Continuing Studies for her popular courses in creative writing, she is co-director of an online writing workshop, www.thewordlounge.com.

COPYRIGHT ACKNOWLEDGMENTS